Kaplan Publishing are constantly finding new ways to support students looking for exam success and our online resources really do add an extra dimension to your studies.

This book comes with free MyKaplan online resources so that you can study anytime, anywhere. **This free online resource is not sold separately and is included in the price of the book.**

Having purchased this book, you have access to the following online study materials:

KU-216-175

CONTENT	AAT	
	Text	Kit
Electronic version of the book	✓	✓
Knowledge Check tests with instant answers	✓	
Mock assessments online	✓	✓
Material updates	✓	✓

How to access your online resources

Kaplan Financial students will already have a MyKaplan account and these extra resources will be available to you online. You do not need to register again, as this process was completed when you enrolled. If you are having problems accessing online materials, please ask your course administrator.

If you are not studying with Kaplan and did not purchase your book via a Kaplan website, to unlock your extra online resources please go to www.mykaplan.co.uk/add-online-resources (even if you have set up an account and registered books previously). You will then need to enter the ISBN number (on the title page and back cover) and the unique pass key number contained in the scratch panel below to gain access. You will also be required to enter additional information during this process to set up or confirm your account details.

If you purchased through the Kaplan Publishing website you will automatically receive an e-mail invitation to MyKaplan. Please register your details using this email to gain access to your content. If you do not receive the e-mail or book content, please contact Kaplan Publishing.

Your Code and Information

This code can only be used once for the registration of one book online. This registration and your online content will expire when the final sittings for the examinations covered by this book have taken place. Please allow one hour from the time you submit your book details for us to process your request.

Please scratch the film to access your unique code.

Please be aware that this code is case-sensitive and you will need to include the dashes within the passcode, but not when entering the ISBN.

KAPLAN

PUBLISHING

ICONS

The chapters include the following icons throughout.

They are designed to assist you in your studies by identifying key definitions and the points at which you can test yourself on the knowledge gained.

 Definition

These sections explain important areas of Knowledge which must be understood and reproduced in an assessment.

 Example

The illustrative examples can be used to help develop an understanding of topics before attempting the activity exercises.

 Test your understanding

These are exercises which give the opportunity to assess your understanding of all the assessment areas.

 Foundation activities

These are questions to help ground your knowledge and consolidate your understanding on areas you're finding tricky.

 Extension activities

These questions are for if you're feeling confident or wish to develop your higher level skills.

Quality and accuracy are of the utmost importance to us so if you spot an error in any of our products, please send an email to mykaplanreporting@kaplan.com with full details.

Our Quality Co-ordinator will work with our technical team to verify the error and take action to ensure it is corrected in future editions.

THE ASSESSMENT

Test specifications for this unit assessment

Assessment type

Computer based assessment

Marking type

Computer marked

Duration of exam

1 hour 30 minutes

Learning outcomes		Weighting
1	Understand the cost recording system within an organisation	30%
2	Use cost recording techniques	40%
3	Provide information on actual and budgeted costs and income	20%
4	Use tools and techniques to support cost calculations	10%
Total		100%

APPENTICESHIP STUDENTS ONLY

UNIT LINK TO THE END POINT ASSESSMENT (EPA)

To achieve the Accounts/Finance Assistant apprenticeship students must pass all of the assessments in the Certificate in Accounting, complete a structured interview supported by a portfolio of evidence summary and the In-tray test.

The In-tray test draws upon knowledge and understanding from the AAT Certificate level. It will be appropriate for students to retain their study materials for individual units until they have successfully completed the In-tray test.

Management accounting compares **actual results with predicted results** and tries to use information to make further predictions about the future.

It also provides information which managers can use to make **decisions**.

Management accounts can be produced in **any format** that is useful to the business and tend to be produced **frequently**, for instance every month.

1.4 The aims of management accounting

The aim of management accounting is to assist management in the following areas of running a business.

- **Planning**

    For example, through the preparation of annual budgets. This is a key aspect of management accounting.

- **Co-ordinating**

    Planning enables all departments to be co-ordinated and to work together.

- **Controlling**

    The comparison of actual results with the budget helps to identify areas where operations are not running according to plan.

    Investigating the causes, and acting on the results of that investigation, helps to control the activities of the business.

- **Communicating**

    Preparing budgets that are distributed to department managers helps to communicate the aims of the business to those managers.

- **Motivating**

    Management accounts include targets. These should motivate managers (and staff) and improve their performance.

    If the target is too difficult, however, it is likely to demotivate and it is unlikely to be achieved.

1.5 Useful management information

For **management information** to be of use to a particular group of managers, it must have the following attributes:

- **Relevant to their responsibilities.** For example, a production manager will want information about inventories, production levels, production performance, etc. within their own department.

- **Relevant to particular decisions.** For example, if deciding whether to close a division, managers would need to know the likely costs including lost sales, likely redundancies and so on.

- **Timely.** Information has to be up to date to be of any value.

- **Value.** The benefits of having the information must outweigh the cost of producing it.

1.6 Cost accounting

Management accounting has **cost accounting** at its essential foundation. As its name suggests, it is concerned with **establishing costs**. It is a system for recording data and producing information about costs for the products produced by an organisation and/or the services it provides. Cost accounting involves a careful evaluation of the resources used within the organisation.

Cost accounting is not confined to the environment of manufacturing, although it is in this area that it is most fully developed. Service industries, central and local government, and accountancy and legal practices also make use of cost accounting information.

Cost accounting is primarily directed at enabling management to perform the fundamental functions of **planning, control** and **decision making:**

(a) determining costs and profits during a control period

(b) valuing inventories of raw materials, work in progress and finished goods, and controlling inventory levels

(c) preparing budgets, forecasts and other control data for a forthcoming control period

(d) creating a reporting system which enables managers to take corrective action where necessary to control costs

(e) providing information for decision-making such as setting the selling price of products or services.

Items (a) and (b) are traditional **cost accounting roles**; (c) to (e) extend into management accounting.

Test your understanding 1

Identify the following statements as being related to planning (P), control (C) or decision making (DM).

	P/ C/ DM
Preparing a forecast for the next 12 month period.	
Making a choice about which new product to launch.	
Comparing actual results for the year with the budget.	

1.7 Differences between management accounting and financial accounting

The following table compares management and cost accounting with financial accounting.

	Management accounting	Financial accounting
Information mainly produced for	Internal use e.g. managers and employees.	External use e.g. shareholders, payables, lenders, banks, government.
Purpose of information	To aid planning, controlling and decision making.	To record the financial performance in a period and the financial position at the end of that period.
Legal requirements	None.	Limited companies must produce financial statements.
Formats	Management decide on the information they require and the most useful way of presenting it.	Format and content of financial accounts should follow accounting standards and company law.
Nature of information	Financial and non-financial.	Mostly financial.
Costing systems	Many different classifications of cost.	Only historic cost.
Time period	Historical and forward-looking.	Mainly a historical record.

Test your understanding 2

The table below lists some of the characteristics of financial accounting and management accounting systems.

Indicate the characteristics for each system by putting a tick in the relevant column of the table.

Characteristic	Financial accounting	Management accounting
Content can include anything useful.	☐	☐
To help managers run the business.	☐	☐
Formats dictated by accounting rules.	☐	☐
Looks mainly at historical information.	☐	☐
Produced for shareholders.	☐	☐

2 Terminology – cost units and cost centres

2.1 Cost units

To help with the above purposes of planning, control and decision making, businesses often need to calculate a cost per unit of output.

A key question, however, is what exactly we mean by a 'unit of output', or **'cost unit'**. This will mean different things to different businesses but we always look at what the business produces.

- A car manufacturer will want to determine the cost of each car and probably different components as well.

- In a printing firm, the cost unit could be the specific customer order.

- For a paint manufacturer, the unit could be a litre of paint.

- An accountancy firm will want to know the costs incurred for each client. To help with this it is common to calculate the cost per hour of chargeable time spent by staff.

- A hospital might wish to calculate the cost per patient treated, the cost of providing a bed for each day or the cost of an operation.

Test your understanding 4

Cost	Cost	Profit	Investment
Human Resource department.	☑	☐	☐
The coffee shop within a large retail store.	☐	☑	☐
The UK division of an organisation which makes its own capital investment decisions.	☐	☐	☑

Test your understanding 5

Characteristic	Financial accounting	Management accounting
Content can include forecasts.	☐	☑
Looks mainly at historical information.	☑	☐
Format must conform to statute and accounting standards.	☑	☐
Any format can be used.	☐	☑
Mainly produced to help managers run and control the business.	☐	☑
Would be used by potential investors thinking of buying shares.	☑	☐
Produced for shareholders.	☑	☐

Test your understanding 6

Characteristic	Financial information	Management information
Report 1 contains a breakdown of the monthly profits by division.	☐	☑
Report 2 was published at Companies House.	☑	☐
Report 3 uses historic and future costs information.	☐	☑

Test your understanding 7

B A production or service location, function, activity or item of equipment for which costs are accumulated

Cost classification

2

Introduction

This chapter explores the different ways in which costs can be classified and used for internal decision making. It also introduces the use of coding in organisations, to ensure that costs and income are allocated to the correct cost, revenue, profit or investment centre and with the correct classification.

ASSESSMENT CRITERIA

Collection and classification of costs in different types of organisations (1.1)

Costing techniques used in organisations (1.2)

Classification and recording of labour and overheads (1.6)

Use cost behaviour to calculate total and unit costs (2.4)

Calculate the costs of a product (2.5)

CONTENTS

1 Cost classification

2 Classification by function

3 Classification by element

4 Classification by nature

5 Classification by behaviour

6 Identifying cost behaviour

7 Coding systems

8 Product and period costs

1 Cost classification

1.1 Purpose of cost classification

Now that we have considered the main cost terms, we need to consider the different classifications of cost that can be used by organisations.

Costs can be **classified** (collected into logical groups) in many ways. The particular classification selected will depend upon the purpose for which the resulting analysed data will be used, for example:

Purpose	Classification
Financial accounts	By **function** – cost of sales, distribution costs, administrative expenses.
Cost control	By **element** – materials, labour, other expenses.
Cost accounts	By **nature** – direct, indirect.
Budgeting, decision making	By **behaviour** – fixed, variable.

Classification of costs will also be determined by the **type of business** being run. For example, fuel for a taxi firm is required for the service they provide, whereas fuel for a delivery vehicle for a manufacturing company is not part of the product they produce. The costs related to fuel would therefore be classified differently by both businesses.

These classifications will be used throughout your study of management accounting. **It is therefore essential that you are familiar with these classifications.**

2 Classification by function

2.1 Cost classification by function

One important classification of costs is by function. For **financial accounting purposes** costs are split into the following categories:

- **Cost of sales** – also known as production costs. This category could include production labour, materials, supervisor salaries and factory rent.

- **Distribution costs** – this includes selling and distribution costs such as sales team commission and delivery costs.

- **Administrative costs** – this includes head office costs, IT support, HR support and so on.

- **Finance** – this refers to money paid to providers of finance (for example banks) and includes bank charges and interest charged on loans.

In manufacturing companies, which much of your studies will cover, the important classification is between production (cost of sales) and non-production costs. Production costs would be incurred in the manufacture of the product. Non-production costs, while not directly involved in the manufacture of the product, are required to support the overall activity of the company. Examples of non-production costs would be distribution, administration and finance costs.

Note that one particular cost you will meet in the exam is **depreciation**. This is a measure of how much an asset is wearing out or being used up. The classification for depreciation will depend on which asset is being depreciated. For example:

- Cost of sales – depreciation on a machine in the production line.

- Distribution – depreciation of a delivery van.

- Admin – depreciation of a computer in the accounts department.

Test your understanding 1

Electronics Ltd makes mobile phones. Classify the following costs by function in the table below.

Cost	Production	Admin	Distribution
Purchases of plastic to make phone cases.	☐	☐	☐
IT director's bonus.	☐	☐	☐
Depreciation of factory building.	☐	☐	☐
Salaries of production workers.	☐	☐	☐
Insurance of sales team laptops.	☐	☐	☐

---

3 Classification by element

3.1 Cost classification by element

The simplest classification you will meet in the exam is splitting costs according to element as follows:

• **Materials** – includes raw materials for a manufacturer or alternatively the cost of goods that are to be resold in a retail organisation.

• **Labour** – labour costs can consist of not only basic pay but overtime, commissions and bonuses as well.

• **Overheads** – this may also be referred to as other expenses and includes electricity, depreciation, rent and so on.

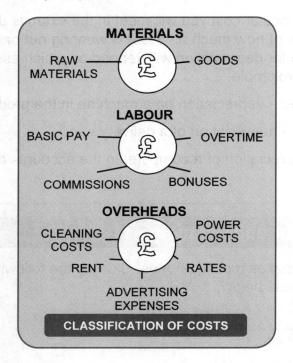

Test your understanding 2

Classify the following costs for a supermarket chain by element in the table below.

Cost	Materials	Labour	Overheads
Tins of baked beans.	☐	☐	☐
Lighting costs.	☐	☐	☐
Depreciation of freezers.	☐	☐	☐
Checkout staff salaries.	☐	☐	☐
Flour used in in-store bakery.	☐	☐	☐

4 Classification by nature

4.1 Cost classification by nature – direct and indirect

To make calculating a cost per unit easier costs are split into the following categories:

- A **direct** cost is an item of cost that is traceable directly to a cost unit.

  An example of direct costs for a furniture manufacturer producing wooden tables might be:

  Direct materials – the cost of the timber, screws and metal drawer handles

  Direct labour – the wages paid to the machine operator, assembler and finisher actually making the table

  Direct expenses – the designer of the table may be entitled to a royalty payment for each table made.

  The total of all direct costs is known as the **'prime cost'** per unit.

- An **indirect** cost is a cost that cannot easily be identified with any one finished unit, although it is clear that it has been incurred in the production of the finished good. Such costs are often referred to as **'overheads'**.

Examples of indirect production costs for the table manufacturer might be:

> **Indirect materials** – lubricating oils for the machines used in production
>
> **Indirect labour** – salaries of factory supervisors
>
> **Indirect expenses** – factory rent and power.

You may notice that we have used the term '**overheads**' in two different ways in the last two sections – once to refer to **expenses** (costs other than labour and materials) when classifying by element, and once to refer to **indirect costs** (costs that can't be traced to individual units of production) when classifying by nature. In reality there are some direct costs that are not materials or labour, but they fall outside the range of this exam. This means that the term 'overhead' can be used to refer to indirect costs **or** expenses.

Test your understanding 3

Chadwicks runs a car repair service and garage. Classify the following costs by nature (direct or indirect) in the table below.

Cost	Direct	Indirect
Engine oil used in services.	☐	☐
Receptionist's wages.	☐	☐
Annual repairs to engine crane.	☐	☐
Brake pads.	☐	☐

Test your understanding 4

Omar Ltd is a furniture manufacturer. Classify the following costs by nature (direct or indirect) in the table below.

Cost	Direct	Indirect
Cost of wood and screws used.	☐	☐
Royalty payable as a result of using a particular chair design.	☐	☐
Oil used to lubricate the machines.	☐	☐
Salesmen's salaries.	☐	☐

5 Classification by behaviour

5.1 Cost classification by behaviour

The final cost classification we will look at is classifying costs depending on their behaviour.

In management accounting, when we talk about cost behaviour we are referring to the way in which **costs vary with differing levels of activity** (i.e. the number of cost units).

An understanding of cost behaviour patterns is essential for many management tasks, particularly in the areas of planning, decision making and control; in particular for **short-term budgeting** purposes.

For example, if a furniture manufacturer expected to produce 1,000 chairs in a particular month, what should the budget be for the costs of wood, labour, oil, selling costs, factory heat and light, manager's salaries, etc.? How would these costs differ (if at all) if it expected to produce 2,000 chairs instead?

To be able to answer such questions and to make budgeting and forecasting easier, costs are split into the following categories of behaviour:

* Variable
* Fixed
* Stepped
* Semi-variable

5.2 Variable costs

Variable costs are costs that vary (usually assumed in direct proportion) with changes in level of activity. Variable costs are **constant per unit** of output and **increase in total in direct proportion to activity**.

For example, if you make twice the number of chairs then the total amount of wood used would double, and hence the **total cost increases proportionally**. This relationship is shown in the first of the following graphs.

The **variable cost per unit would remain the same**, as the cost of the wood needed in each chair is the same. This is shown in the second of the following graphs.

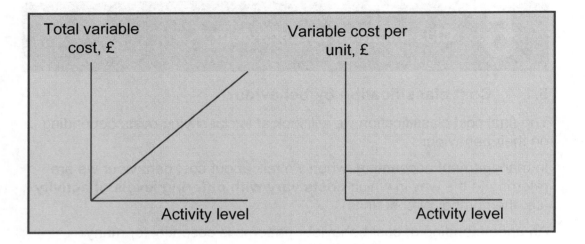

Example 1

If a business has total variable costs of £20,000 when it produces 1,000 units what is the variable cost per unit?

£20,000/1,000 = £20

What would be the total variable cost if the activity increased to 3,000 units?

£20 × 3,000 = £60,000

5.3 Fixed costs

Fixed costs are costs that, in the short term, are not affected by changes in activity level. The **total cost stays constant** as activity levels change. For example, the rent on the factory. This is shown in the first of the following graphs.

The **fixed cost per unit reduces as the activity levels in increased**. This is because the same amount of fixed cost is being spread over an increasing number of units. This is shown in the second of the following graphs.

Note that the graph showing the variable cost per unit looks exactly the same as the total fixed cost graph. It is therefore always important to check the vertical axis on the graph as these two are easily confused.

KAPLAN PUBLISHING

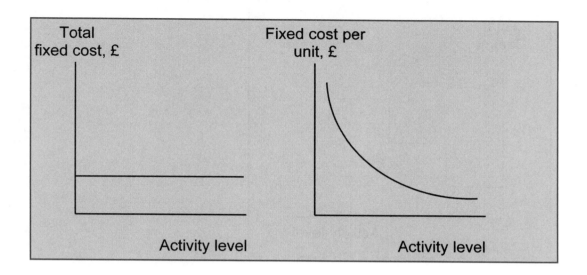

Example 2

If a business has total fixed costs of £30,000 when it produces 10,000 units what is the fixed cost per unit?

£30,000/10,000 = £3

If a business has total fixed costs of £30,000 when it produces 20,000 units what is the fixed cost per unit?

£30,000/20,000 = £1.50

What would be the total fixed cost if the activity increased to 30,000 units?

£30,000

5.4 Stepped costs

Stepped costs are costs that remain fixed up to a particular level of activity, but which rise to a higher (fixed) level if activity goes beyond that range.

For example, a firm may pay £40,000 per year to rent a factory in which they can produce up to 1 million units of product per year. However, if demand increases to more than 1 million units a second factory may be required, in which case the cost of factory rent may step up to, say, £80,000 per year and then be constant until we want to make in excess of 2 million units.

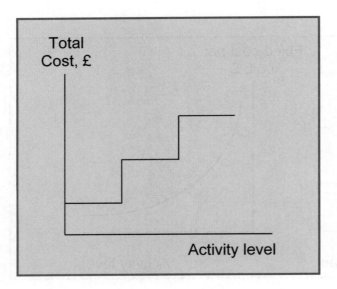

5.5   Semi-variable costs

Semi-variable costs are those that have a fixed element **and** a variable element. Examples of semi-variable costs are:

- gas
- electricity
- telephone

These costs consist of a fixed amount payable for the period regardless of the level of use (such as a standing charge), with a further variable amount which is related to consumption of gas or electricity, or the number of telephone calls made.

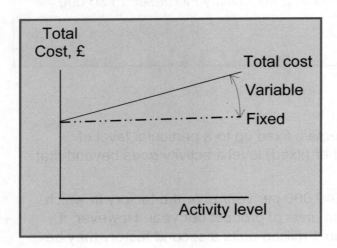

It therefore stands to reason that **Total semi-variable costs = Fixed costs + Variable costs**

Or alternatively, **Total semi-variable costs = Fixed costs + (Variable cost per unit × number of units).**

Test your understanding 5

The Grande is a hotel in Sri Lanka. Classify the following costs by their behaviour in the table below.

Cost	Fixed	Variable	Semi-variable
Manager's salary.	☐	☐	☐
Cleaning materials.	☐	☐	☐
Food served in the restaurant.	☐	☐	☐
Electricity – includes a standing charge.	☐	☐	☐
Cleaner's wages (paid per room cleaned).	☐	☐	☐

Test your understanding 6

Which of the following best describes a 'pure' fixed cost?

A cost which:

A   represents a fixed proportion of total costs

B   remains at the same level up to a particular level of output

C   has a direct relationship with output

D   remains at the same level whenever output changes

Test your understanding 7

Identify the following statements as either true or false in the table below.

	True	False
Semi-variable costs have a fixed and variable element.	☐	☐
Total fixed costs change directly with changes in activity.	☐	☐
Total variable costs change directly with changes in activity.	☐	☐

6 Identifying cost behaviour

6.1 Identifying cost behaviour

The behavioural characteristics of costs will be of particular use to management accountants for the purpose of budgeting and forecasting what the business' costs will be in future periods.

When producing a budget or forecast it may be necessary to identify the type of behaviour a cost is exhibiting. It is useful to remember the following:

- Fixed costs are constant in total

- Variable costs are constant per unit

- Semi-variable costs are neither constant per unit nor constant in total.

Example 3

A company has a mix of variable, semi-variable and fixed costs. Identify the behaviour for each of the costs shown below.

	Total cost @ 1,500 units	Total cost @ 2,500 units
Materials	£15,000	£25,000
Rent	£34,000	£34,000
Electricity	£33,500	£42,500

Materials is a **variable cost**.

At 1,500 units the cost per unit is £15,000/1,500 = £10 per unit. At 2,500 units the cost per unit is £25,000/2,500 = £10 per unit.

Rent is a **fixed cost**.

The total cost does not change as the activity level changes.

Electricity is a **semi-variable cost**.

The total cost changes when the activity level changes and so the cost is not fixed. The cost per unit at the lower activity level is £33,500/1,500 = £22.33 per unit and at the higher activity level is £42,500/2,500 = £17 per unit. The cost per unit is therefore not constant and this is not a variable cost. It must therefore be a semi-variable cost.

Test your understanding 8

Identify the type of cost behaviour (fixed, variable or semi-variable) described in each statement below, by putting a tick in the relevant column of the table.

	Fixed	Variable	Semi-variable
Total costs are £45,000 when 22,500 units are made and £60,000 when 30,000 units are made.	☐	☐	☐
Unit costs are £5 per unit when 8,000 units are made and £1.25 when 32,000 units are made.	☐	☐	☐
Total costs are £30,000 when 10,000 units are made and £40,000 when 18,000 units are made.	☐	☐	☐

6.2 Combining cost classifications

In some tasks in your assessment you may have to use more than one classification at a time. For example

- Factory rent is a production cost that is fixed (or stepped) and indirect.

- Direct materials are a production cost that is also variable.

- Direct labour is not necessarily a variable cost. For a car repair service, for example, it is possible to identify how much time a particular repair takes (by using job cards to record time) but the mechanic may be on a fixed salary per month.

- Sales commission is a variable selling and distribution cost.

📝 Test your understanding 9

Identify the following statements as either true or false in the table below.

	True	False
All direct costs are variable.	☐	☐
All overheads are fixed.	☐	☐
Depreciation is always classified as an administrative cost.	☐	☐
All selling costs are fixed.	☐	☐

6.3 Why do organisations need to classify costs in different ways?

As you have seen in the previous sections, costs can be classified by nature, element, behaviour, or by function. Why do organisations need these different classifications?

The answer is that the different classifications will be used by the organisation for different purposes.

- **Classifying costs by element or nature** (materials, labour or overheads/direct and indirect costs) will be particularly useful for management accountants to help the business calculate how much each unit of product has cost to make. This can help the business decide how much to sell the product for.

- **Classifying costs by behaviour** (fixed, variable, stepped or semi-variable) will also be of use to management accountants, especially for the purpose of budgeting what the business' costs will be in future periods. For instance, if the business expects to double the number of units it makes next year, it will know that this will not affect the level of fixed costs, but would expect to double variable costs.

- **Classifying costs by function** (production, selling and distribution or administration) is of particular use to financial accountants, as it will help them to see the overall level of expenditure in each part of the organisation and therefore calculate total profit levels. This will then form part of the organisation's year-end financial accounts – in particular the income statement.

7 Coding systems

7.1 Coding systems

Cost accountants need to determine the costs that relate to each cost, profit or investment centre. To make this simpler, each expense is classified according to its cost centre and type of expense.

When an invoice is received by the organisation it will undergo a variety of checks to ensure that it is for valid purchases that were ordered and have been received or that it is for a service that has been received.

In the process of these checks it will become clear what type of goods or service is being dealt with, for example it may be an invoice for the purchase of raw materials for the factory or an electricity bill for the entire organisation.

Once the invoice has been checked for validity then it must be correctly coded. A **cost code** will be allocated to the expense to represent this classification before it is entered on to the accounting system.

Definition

A **code** is a system of symbols designed to be applied to a classified set of items, to give a brief, accurate reference, which helps entry to the records, collation and analysis.

A cost code is a code used in a costing system.

7.2 Cost codes

In general, cost codes are constructed by deciding on the information that is needed. For most businesses we want to identify

(a) the responsibility centre (cost/ revenue/ profit/ investment) that is incurring the cost and

(b) the type of cost that is incurred.

There are **no set methods** of designing a cost code and the cost code of a particular organisation will be that which **best suits** the operations and costs of that business.

For example, if a business has only one division/operating centre, then there will be no need to identify that centre in the cost code. But if a business has several divisions, then the division that incurs the cost will need to be identified in the cost code.

Similarly, if the divisions have several cost centres and incur several different types of cost, then the cost code must be able to identify each of these.

There are a number of different methods of coding data:

*   **numeric,** e.g. 100/310

*   **alphabetic,** e.g. AB/RT

*   **alphanumeric**, e.g. A230

Example 4

Consider a company that has two operating divisions (North and South), two cost centres in each division (Construction and Despatch) with each cost centre incurring three types of cost (material, labour and expenses).

A typical cost code could be devised as follows:

Step 1

Decide the structure of the cost code, for example **/**/**, where

First two digits	the operating division
Second two digits	the cost centre
Third two digits	the type of cost

Step 2

Allocate code numbers to the elements

      (a)   two operating divisions

North 01

South 02

      (b)   each division has two cost centres

Construction 01

Despatch 02

      (c)   each cost centre incurs three types of cost

Materials 01

Labour 02

Expenses 03

Examples

Thus a cost code for expenses incurred by the despatch centre of the North division would be:

First two digits	the operating division	North	01
Second two digits	the cost centre	Despatch	02
Third two digits	the type of cost	Expenses	03

The cost code would therefore be: 01/02/03

Similarly, the code for materials purchased by the construction centre of the South would be 02/01/01.

Test your understanding 10

Safety Ltd manufactures motorbike helmets.

It has two factories that are coded as:

Slough	S
Leeds	L

Each factory has the following cost centres:

Machining	120
Finishing	121
Packing	122
Stores	123
Canteen	124
Maintenance	125
Administration	126

Type of expense:

Labour	200
Material	201
Expenses	202

Sales revenue:	210

Thus, the cost of production labour in the Finishing Department at the Leeds factory would be coded L/121/200.

Code the following expenses using the table below.

Transaction	Code
Slough factory, cleaning materials used in the canteen.	
Slough factory, wages for stores personnel.	
Leeds factory, electricity for machining department.	
Leeds factory, telephone account for site as a whole.	
Slough factory, general maintenance material for repairs.	

Test your understanding 11

Maxim Ltd, a manufacturer of garden lighting, uses a numerical coding structure based on one profit centre and three cost centres as outlined below. Each code has a sub-code so each transaction will be coded as ***/***.

Profit/cost centre	Code	Sub-classification	Sub-code
Sales	100	Sales to the public	100
		Sales to retailers	200
Production	200	Direct costs	100
		Indirect costs	200
Selling and distribution	300	Direct costs	100
		Indirect costs	200
Administration	400	Direct costs	100
		Indirect costs	200

Code the following revenue and expense transactions, which have been extracted from purchase invoices, sales invoices and payroll, using the table below.

Transaction	Code
Wages for staff working in the factory canteen.	
Sales to a French retailer.	
Sales to individuals via the company website.	
Depreciation on cars provided to salesmen.	
Bulbs for use in the garden lighting products.	
Chief accountant's salary.	

7.3 Purpose of cost codes

The main purposes of cost codes are to:

- **assist precise information:** costs incurred can be associated with pre-established codes, so reducing variations in classification

- **facilitate electronic data processing:** computer analysis, summarisation and presentation of data can be performed more easily through the use of codes

- **facilitate a logical and systematic arrangement of costing records:** accounts can be arranged in blocks of codes permitting additional codes to be inserted in logical order

- **simplify comparison of totals of similar expenses** rather than all of the individual items

- **incorporate check codes** within the main code to check the accuracy of the postings.

8 Product and period costs

8.1 Cost cards

One of the aims of costing is to help the business calculate how much each unit of product has cost to make or the service has cost to provide. The management accountant can use this information to help make short-term decisions, such as how much to sell the product or service for.

We can use a cost card to show the breakdown of the costs of producing goods/services, based on the chosen classification of each cost.

The following cost card is an example of a cost card for one unit.

Direct costs	£
Direct materials (3kg @ £5 per kg)	15
Direct labour (4 hours @ £10 per hour)	40
Direct expenses	12
	___
Prime cost (total of direct costs)	**67**
Overheads (indirect costs)	15
	___
Total product cost	**82**

8.2 Product and period costs

The costs included in the cost card are known as **product costs**. A product cost is a cost that relates to the product or service being produced or provided, e.g. raw materials. Product costs are **charged to the individual product or service** and matched against the sales revenue they generate. Product costs might be fixed or variable. Variable product costs would be easily identified, such as material and labour costs. Fixed product costs might include costs such as an assembly line supervisor's annual salary. A cost such as this will be included within the 'overheads' section of the job card. This process of overhead apportionment will be covered in a later chapter.

Period costs are costs that relate to a particular time period as opposed to a particular product or service. These include costs such as administrative costs, selling and distribution costs and finance costs. Period costs are **charged in full to the statement of profit or loss** in the period in which they are incurred.

In the study text chapters which follow we will learn how to calculate the different components of product cost seen in the above cost card, starting with the cost of materials in chapter 3.

📝 Test your understanding 12

Classify the following costs as being product or period costs.

Cost	Product	Period
Chief Executive's annual salary.	☐	☐
Raw materials used in production.	☐	☐
Assembly line supervisor.	☐	☐
Depreciation of delivery vehicles.	☐	☐
Market research.	☐	☐
Production department protective equipment.	☐	☐

---

9 Summary

In this chapter we have seen that costs can be classified in a variety of different ways for different purposes. The basic classification by **element** is into **materials, labour** and **expenses**, each of which will be dealt with in detail in the following chapters.

A further method of classification by **nature** is into **direct and indirect** costs.

For short-term decision-making and budgeting purposes, it is often useful to distinguish costs according to their **behaviour** as production levels change. The basic classifications according to behaviour are **fixed** and **variable** costs although there are also **stepped** costs and **semi-variable** costs.

You should also now know the importance of coding of costs and income. If actual costs and income are to be used for management purposes then it is vital that they are correctly classified and coded to ensure that they are allocated to the correct cost, revenue, profit or investment centre and according to the correct type of costs. Only then can any useful management information be obtained.

Finally, it is also important to be able to distinguish **product** and **period** costs and to understand the different treatment of these costs.

10 Further Test your understanding exercises

Test your understanding 13

Zenawi plc makes garden furniture.

Classify the following costs by function in the table below.

Cost	Production	Admin	Distribution
Purchases of wood to make chairs.	☐	☐	☐
Depreciation of delivery vans.	☐	☐	☐
HR director's bonus.	☐	☐	☐
Salaries of production workers.	☐	☐	☐
Electricity bill for workshop.	☐	☐	☐
Insurance of sales team laptops.	☐	☐	☐

Test your understanding 14

Kim and Yoshiro are the founding partners of an accountancy firm. They employ 20 accountants and have over 100 clients.

Classify the following costs by nature (direct or indirect) in the table below.

Cost	Direct	Indirect
Travelling costs for when staff visit clients.	☐	☐
Rechargeable accountants' time.	☐	☐
Office heating costs.	☐	☐
Recruitment costs.	☐	☐
Accountants' time recorded as 'general admin.' on time sheets.	☐	☐

Test your understanding 15

Elite Cars is a family-run business specialising in the sale, hire, servicing and repair of classic cars.

Classify the following costs by their behaviour in the table below.

Cost	Fixed	Variable	Semi-variable
Sales staff pay (basic salary plus commission per car sold).	☐	☐	☐
Motor oil used in servicing.	☐	☐	☐
Depreciation of premises.	☐	☐	☐
Mechanics' pay (salaried).	☐	☐	☐
Electricity.	☐	☐	☐

Test your understanding 16

Complete the following statement be selecting one of the options in bold for each missing answer.

As the units of production decrease, the unit cost **[increases/ decreases]** because **[fixed/ variable]** costs remain the same at all levels.

KAPLAN PUBLISHING

Test your understanding 17

Ink plc manufactures computer printers and wishes to start coding its costs. It has decided to use an alphabetic code, based on the nature and the element of each cost, as well as the function it relates to.

The first part of the code will depend on whether the cost is direct or indirect.

Direct	J
Indirect	F

The second part of the code will depend on whether the cost is materials, labour or overheads (expenses).

Labour	HF
Materials	MB
Overheads	VV

The third part of the code will depend on the function that the cost relates to.

Production	PR
Administration	AD
Sales and distribution	SD

Thus, the cost of indirect production materials would be coded F/MB/PR

Code the following expenses using the table below.

Transaction	Code
Purchase of plastic used in the production of printers.	
Electricity used in Ink's administration head office.	
Wages paid to the cleaner of Ink's delivery vans.	
Purchase of ink for the head office printers.	
Salary paid to Ink's factory supervisor.	

Test your understanding 18

A company manufactures shoes and slippers in half-sizes in the following size ranges:

- Men 6 to 9½
- Ladies 3 to 9
- Boys 1 to 5½
- Girls 1 to 5

The company uses a seven-digit code to identify its finished products, which, reading from left to right, is built up as follows:

Digit one indicates whether the products are men, ladies, boys or girls. The numbers used are

1	–	men
2	–	ladies
3	–	boys
4	–	girls

Digit two denotes type of footwear (3 is shoes; 6 is slippers)

Digit three denotes colour (5 is green; 6 is burgundy, 1 is brown)

Digit four denotes the material of the upper part of the product (leather is 4, suede is 3)

Digit five denotes the material of the sole (leather is 1, 2 is rubber)

Digits six and seven denote size.

Example

Code 1613275 represents a pair of Men's slippers, brown suede, rubber sole, size 7½.

Task: Set suitable code numbers to the following:

Product	Code
Boys' shoes, brown leather uppers, rubber soles, size 4.	
Ladies' slippers, green suede uppers, rubber soles, size 4½.	
Girls' shoes, burgundy leather uppers, leather soles, size 3½.	

Test your understanding 19

The expenses of an international organisation are coded with a seven digit code system as follows:

First and second digits   –   location
Third and fourth digits   –   function
Final three digits   –   type of expense

Extracts from within the costing system are as follows:

Location	Code	Function	Code
London	10	Production	20
Dublin	11	Marketing	21
Lagos	12	Accounts	23
Nairobi	13	Administration	24
Kuala Lumpur	17		
Hong Kong	18	**Type of expense**	**Code**
		Factory rent	201
		Stationery	202
		Telephone	203
		Travel	204
		Entertainment	205

Examples of the codes are as follows:

Factory rent in Nairobi: 1320201
Stationery purchased in London office: 1024202

Task

Code the following revenue and expense transactions, which have been extracted from purchase invoices, sales invoices and payroll, using the table below.

Transaction	Code
Factory rent in the Dublin factory.	
Administration telephone costs incurred in Lagos.	
Sales person in Hong Kong entertaining an overseas visitor.	
Marketing brochures ordered in London.	

Test your understanding answers

Test your understanding 1

Cost	Production	Admin	Distribution
Purchases of plastic to make phone cases.	☑	☐	☐
IT director's bonus.	☐	☑	☐
Depreciation of factory building.	☑	☐	☐
Salaries of production workers.	☑	☐	☐
Insurance of sales team laptops.	☐	☐	☑

Test your understanding 2

Cost	Materials	Labour	Overheads
Tins of baked beans.	☑	☐	☐
Lighting costs.	☐	☐	☑
Depreciation of freezers.	☐	☐	☑
Checkout staff salaries.	☐	☑	☐
Flour used in in-store bakery.	☑	☐	☐

KAPLAN PUBLISHING

Test your understanding 3

Cost	Direct	Indirect
Engine oil used in services.	☑	☐
Receptionist's wages.	☐	☑
Annual repairs to engine crane.	☐	☑
Brake pads.	☑	☐

Test your understanding 4

Cost	Direct	Indirect
Cost of wood and screws used.	☑	☐
Royalty payable as a result of using a particular chair design.	☑	☐
Oil used to lubricate the machines.	☐	☑
Salesmen's salaries.	☐	☑

Note: You may have argued that oil was direct as you could calculate how much oil is needed per item made. However, it would be very difficult to determine the oil need for a **particular** item of furniture; hence the correct answer is indirect.

Test your understanding 5

Cost	Fixed	Variable	Semi-variable
Manager's salary.	☑	☐	☐
Cleaning materials.	☐	☑	☐
Food served in the restaurant.	☐	☑	☐
Electricity – includes a standing charge.	☐	☐	☑
Cleaner's wages (paid per room cleaned).	☐	☑	☐

Test your understanding 6

D – Pure fixed costs remain exactly the same in total regardless of the activity level.

Test your understanding 7

	True	False
Semi-variable costs have a fixed and variable element.	☑	☐
Total fixed costs change directly with changes in activity.	☐	☑
Total variable costs change directly with changes in activity.	☑	☐

KAPLAN PUBLISHING

Test your understanding 8

	Fixed	Variable	Semi-variable
Total costs are £45,000 when 22,500 units are made and £60,000 when 30,000 units are made.	☐	☑	☐
Unit costs are £5 per unit when 8,000 units are made and £1.25 when 32,000 units are made.	☑	☐	☐
Total costs are £30,000 when 10,000 units are made and £40,000 when 18,000 units are made.	☐	☐	☑

£45,000 ÷ 22,500 units = £2 per unit, £60,000 ÷ 30,000 units = £2 per unit. **Cost per unit is constant at different activity levels, which indicates a variable cost.**

Cost per unit is different at each activity level and so it is not a variable cost. Find the total cost at each activity level next to determine whether it is a fixed cost. 8,000 units × £5 = £40,000, 32,000 units × £1.25 = £40,000. **Total cost is constant at different activity levels, which indicates a fixed cost.**

Total cost is different at different activity levels and so this is not a fixed cost. Find the cost per unit to see if it is a variable cost. £30,000 ÷ 10,000 units = £3 per unit, £40,000 ÷ 18,000 units = £2.22, therefore it is not a variable cost. It must therefore be a **semi-variable** cost.

Test your understanding 9

	True	False
All direct costs are variable.	☐	☑ Note 1
All overheads are fixed.	☐	☑ Note 2
Depreciation is always classified as an administrative cost.	☐	☑ Note 3
All selling costs are fixed.	☐	☑ Note 4

Note 1   Whereas direct materials are usually variable, direct labour may be fixed – e.g. lawyers may be on a fixed salary but produce detailed timesheets so a direct labour cost can be calculated for each client.

Note 2   Electricity is usually classified as an overhead but will have a variable element. If more units are made on a production line, then more electricity will be used (hence variable). However, it may not be possible or practical to measure exactly how much electricity is used to make a particular unit (hence indirect).

Note 3   For example, depreciation on production machinery would be included in cost of sales.

Note 4   Sales commission would be a variable selling cost.

Test your understanding 10

Transaction	Code
Slough factory, cleaning materials used in the canteen.	S/124/201
Slough factory, wages for stores personnel.	S/123/200
Leeds factory, electricity for Machining Department.	L/120/202
Leeds factory, telephone account for site as a whole.	L/126/202
Slough factory, general maintenance material for repairs.	S/125/201

Test your understanding 11

Transaction	Code
Wages for staff working in the factory canteen.	200/200
Sales to a French retailer.	100/200
Sales to individuals via the company website.	100/100
Depreciation on cars provided to salesmen.	300/200
Bulbs for use in the garden lighting products.	200/100
Chief accountant's salary.	400/200

Test your understanding 12

Cost	Product	Period
Chief Executive annual salary.	☐	☑
Raw materials used in production.	☑	☐
Assembly line supervisor.	☑	☐
Depreciation of delivery vehicles.	☐	☑
Market research.	☐	☑
Production department protective equipment.	☑	☐

Test your understanding 13

Cost	Production	Admin	Distribution
Purchases of wood to make chairs.	☑	☐	☐
Depreciation of delivery vans.	☐	☐	☑
HR director's bonus.	☐	☑	☐
Salaries of production workers.	☑	☐	☐
Electricity bill for workshop.	☑	☐	☐
Insurance of sales team laptops.	☐	☐	☑

Test your understanding 14

Cost	Direct	Indirect
Travelling costs for when staff visit clients.	☑	☐
Rechargeable accountants' time.	☑	☐
Office heating costs.	☐	☑
Recruitment costs.	☐	☑
Accountants' time recorded as 'general admin.' on time sheets.	☐	☑

KAPLAN PUBLISHING

Test your understanding 15

Cost	Fixed	Variable	Semi-variable
Sales staff pay (basic salary plus commission per car sold).	☐	☐	☑
Motor oil used in servicing.	☐	☑	☐
Depreciation of premises.	☑	☐	☐
Mechanics' pay (salaried).	☑	☐	☐
Electricity.	☐	☐	☑

Test your understanding 16

As the units of production decrease, the unit cost **increases** because **fixed** costs remain the same at all levels.

The fixed costs remain the same regardless of the level of activity. Therefore the higher the activity level, the lower the fixed cost per unit, as the total fixed costs are being spread over more units.
If production decreases, then the fixed costs are being spread over fewer units, resulting in a higher fixed cost per unit. This will increase the unit cost.

Test your understanding 17

Transaction	Code
Purchase of plastic used in the production of printers.	J/MB/PR
Electricity used in Jian's administration head office.	F/VV/AD
Wages paid to the cleaner of Jian's delivery vans.	F/HF/SD
Purchase of ink for the head office printers.	F/MB/AD
Salary paid to Jian's factory supervisor.	F/HF/PR

Test your understanding 18

Product	Code
Boys' shoes, brown leather uppers, rubber soles, size 4.	3314240
Ladies slippers, green suede uppers, rubber soles, size 4½.	2653245
Girls' shoes, burgundy leather uppers, leather soles, size 3½.	4364135

(i)   Boys shoes, brown leather uppers, rubber soles, size 4.

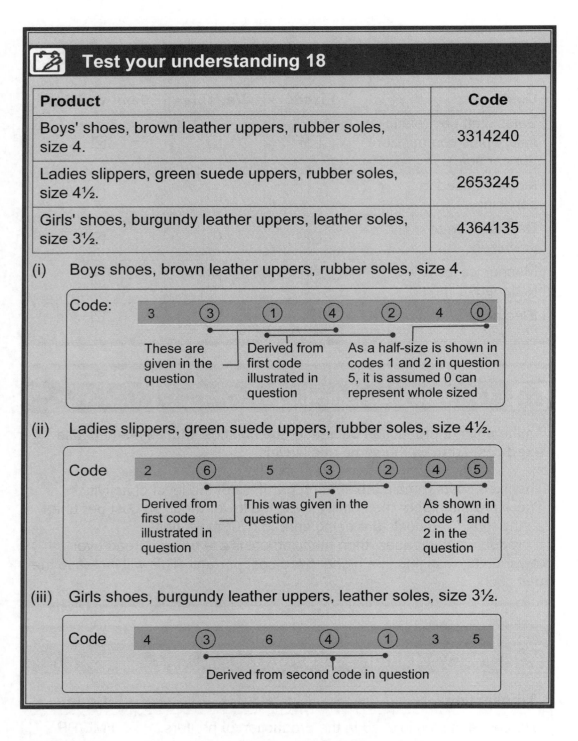

(ii)   Ladies slippers, green suede uppers, rubber soles, size 4½.

(iii)   Girls shoes, burgundy leather uppers, leather soles, size 3½.

Test your understanding 19

Transaction	Code
Factory rent in the Dublin factory.	1120201
Administration telephone costs incurred in Lagos.	1224203
Sales person in Hong Kong entertaining an overseas visitor.	1821205
Marketing brochures ordered in London.	1021202

Materials and inventory

3

Introduction

In this chapter we begin to build up the product cost seen in previous chapters, starting with the cost of materials. We start by considering the different types of inventory that an organisation might hold and learn how to place a value on those inventories when they are issued to production. This value becomes the 'material cost' in our product cost card. We will also look at how we value our closing inventories at the end of a period and consider inventory control policy.

In a manufacturing business, inventory (materials) may be the largest item of cost. This chapter looks at how we calculate the costs of products in manufacturing organisations, using a manufacturing account.

ASSESSMENT CRITERIA	CONTENTS
Costing techniques used in organisations (1.2)	1 Different types of inventory
Classification and recording of labour and overheads (1.6)	2 Valuing raw materials
Calculate cost of inventory issues and inventory valuations (2.1)	3 Manufacturing accounts
Calculate the costs of a product (2.5)	4 Inventory control

1 Different types of inventory

1.1 The production cycle

For a retailer the main type of inventory will be goods bought for resale. For example, a supermarket will buy goods from its supplier which it then sells on to the end consumer.

For a manufacturer, however, we can identify three different types of inventory:

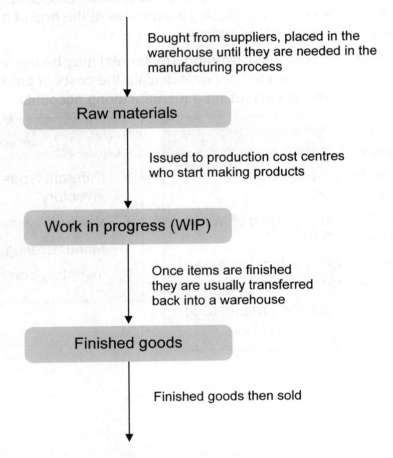

Bought from suppliers, placed in the warehouse until they are needed in the manufacturing process

Raw materials

Issued to production cost centres who start making products

Work in progress (WIP)

Once items are finished they are usually transferred back into a warehouse

Finished goods

Finished goods then sold

You may also see 'inventory' referred to as 'stock'.

1.2 Materials

For manufacturing organisations, various raw materials are needed to make the main product of the business.

Remember that, for management accounting purposes, costs can be classified as either direct or indirect. Materials are no exception to this.

Definition

Direct materials are the materials that are used directly as part of the production of the goods that the organisation makes.

The direct materials are therefore the raw materials that are part of the manufacturing process. For example, in a business that makes wooden furniture, the direct materials would include wood, screws and polish.

 Definition

Indirect materials are other materials used in the production process which are not used in the actual products themselves.

So, for example, lubricant for the machines that make the wooden furniture would be classified as indirect materials as it would be extremely difficult to identify how much lubricant was used to make a particular chair, say.

 Definition

The total **direct** cost for a product (the direct materials, direct labour and direct expenses) is sometimes referred to as the **prime cost**.

1.3   Work in progress

Work in progress (WIP) refers to units that have been started but are incomplete at the end of the accounting period.

For example a wooden table may have had the top made but is still waiting for legs to be attached.

1.4   Finished goods

Finished goods are completed and ready for selling to customers.

The procedure for valuing WIP and finished goods will be covered in the later chapter on 'Overhead absorption'.

2 Valuing raw materials

2.1 Introduction

There are two aspects to valuing raw materials:

- **Costing.** Firstly we need to determine the cost of materials issued to production cost centres, to include on the **cost card** for the unit.

- **Financial reporting**. Secondly we need to be able to value the inventory of raw materials left in stores, to include in the financial statements.

The cost of materials to include in our product cost will normally be derived from suppliers' invoices as the purchase amount, but, where many purchases have been made at differing prices, a decision has to be taken as to which cost is used when inventory is issued to the user department (cost centre).

Example 1

Petra Ltd has the following movements in a certain type of inventory into and out of its stores for the month of May:

Date	Receipts			Issues	
	Kg	Price/kg	Cost	Kg	Cost
May 1	200	£9.00	£1,800		
May 2	100	£10.80	£1,080		
May 3				50	?

What is the cost of materials issued on May 3?

Should we use £9/kg, £10.80/kg or something in between?

2.2 Methods of pricing issues of materials

Various methods exist, including:

(a) FIFO (first in, first out)

(b) LIFO (last in, first out)

(c) Weighted average (AVCO)

The choice of method will not only affect the charge to the user department for which the material is required (the value of materials charged to the **product cost**), but also the value of the **inventory** left in stores.

These systems attempt to reflect the movements of individual units in to and out of inventory, under different assumptions.

FIFO

- Assumes that inventory issues to production will be made from the oldest inventory available.

- Issues will therefore be made at the oldest prices. In times of rising prices (e.g. with inflation) the issues, and therefore the materials cost on the cost card, will be at the lowest price. This will result in a lower product cost.

- Closing inventory will be made up of the latest purchases. These will be valued at the newest prices which, where prices are rising, will result in a higher value for closing inventory.

- FIFO is particularly useful when products are perishable and you want the oldest used first to avoid it going off or becoming out of date e.g. milk.

LIFO

- Assumes that inventory issues to production will be made from the newest inventory available

- Issues will be therefore be made at the most recent prices. In times of rising prices (e.g. with inflation) the issues, and therefore the materials cost on the cost card, will be at the highest price. This will result in a higher product cost.

- Closing inventory will be made up of the earliest purchases. These will be valued at the older prices which, where prices are rising, will result in a lower value for closing inventory.

- LIFO could be used when products are not perishable e.g. stationery.

AVCO

- Assumes that the issues into production will be made at an average price:

$$\text{Average price per unit} = \frac{\text{Total value of inventory}}{\text{Total units in inventory}}$$

- A new average cost is calculated before each issue to production.

- AVCO could be used when individual units of material are not separately definable e.g. liquids, such as petrol. With petrol, when a tank gets topped up, the new petrol is mixed with old petrol.

Example 1 – continued

Petra Ltd has the following movements in a certain type of inventory into and out of it stores for the month of May:

Date	Receipts			Issues	
	Kg	Price/kg	Cost	Kg	Cost
May 1	200	£9.00	£1,800		
May 2	100	£10.80	£1,080		
May 3				50	

Complete the table below for the issue and closing inventory values.

Method	Cost of issue	Closing inventory
FIFO		
LIFO		
AVCO		

Solution

Method	Cost of issue	Closing inventory
FIFO	£450	£2,430
LIFO	£540	£2,340
AVCO	£480	£2,400

LIFO

- The 50 kg issued on May 3rd will all come from the **most recent** purchase made on May 2nd

- Thus the cost of the issue will be 50 kg @ £10.80 = £540

- Closing inventory = £2,880 – £540 = £2,340

- **OR** closing inventory will be 200 kg @ £9 (May 1st purchase) and 50 kg @ £10.80 (the remaining inventory from May 2nd) = £2,340

AVCO

- We bought 300 kg at a total cost of (200 kg @ £9) + (100 kg @ £10.80) = £2,880

- On average this works out at £2,880/300 kg = £9.60/kg

- Thus the cost of the issue will be 50 kg @ £9.60 = £480

- Closing inventory = £2,880 – £480 = £2,400

- **OR** closing inventory carried forwards will have the same average cost per unit so will be 250 kg @ £9.60 = £2,400

Test your understanding 1

Krully Ltd has the following movements in a certain type of inventory into and out of its stores for the month of June:

Date	Receipts		Issues	
	Units	Cost	Units	Cost
June 2	100	£400		
June 3	200	£1,000		
June 6	200	£1,200		
June 19			400	
June 25	400	£2,500		

Complete the table below for the issue and closing inventory values.

Method	Cost of issue on 19 June	Closing inventory at 30 June
FIFO		
LIFO		
AVCO		

Test your understanding 2

Jetty Ltd has opening inventory of raw material X of 1,500 units at £2 per unit. In the month another 1,000 units at £4.50 are received and the following week 1,800 units are issued.

Identify whether the statements in the table below are true or false by putting a tick in the relevant column.

Statement	True	False
FIFO values the closing inventory at £1,400.	☐	☐
LIFO costs the issue at £6,100.	☐	☐
AVCO costs the issue at £5,400.	☐	☐

2.3 Determining which method of inventory valuation has been used

You may be given a completed or partially completed inventory card and asked to decide which of the three methods have been used to produce it.

 Example 2

JJJ Ltd has the following movements in a certain type of inventory into and out of it stores for the month of June:

Date	Receipts			Issues	
	Kg	Price/kg	Cost	Kg	Cost
June 1	500	£5.00	£2,500		
June 2	700	£6.00	£4,200		
June 3				900	£4,900

Identify the method JJJ has used to value its inventory and calculate the valuation of closing inventory using this method.

Solution

Method	Closing inventory
FIFO	£1,800

Workings

Identifying the method used to value closing inventory:

The most reliable way of tackling this question is to look at the cost calculation that has been done for you – in this case the cost of the issue on June 3rd. If we calculate what this issue would be worth under each of the three valuation methods, we should be able to identify the approach that JJJ has taken.

LIFO

- The 900 kg issued on June 3rd will all come from the **most recent** purchases made.

- Thus the cost of the issue will be (700 kg @ £6) + (200 kg @ £5) = £5,200.

- As the cost of the issue is £4,900, the method being used is not LIFO.

AVCO

- We bought 1,200 kg at a total cost of (500 kg @ £5) + (700 kg @ £6) = £6,700

- On average this works out at £6,700/1,200 = £5.58/kg

- Thus the cost of the issue will be 900 kg @ £5.58/kg = £5,022

- As the cost of the issue is £4,900, the method being used is not AVCO.

FIFO

- The 900 kg issued on June 3rd will all come from the **earliest** purchases.

- Thus the cost of the issue will be (500 kg @ £5) + (400 kg @ £6) = £4,900. As this is the value of the issue given, FIFO must be the valuation method used.

Calculating the value of closing inventory using this method:

- Remember that there are two ways to get closing inventory.

- The first is to look at the flow of units: closing inventory will be 300 kg @ £6 (the remaining inventory from the June 2nd purchase).

- The second approach, which will probably be easier in the exam, is to consider total purchases and simply deduct issues. Total purchases = £6,700, so closing inventory = £6,700 – £4,900 = £1,800.

Test your understanding 3

Flotsam Ltd has opening inventory of raw material P of 3,000 units at £4.50 per unit. In the month another 2,000 units at £7 are received and the following week 3,750 units are issued.

Identify the valuation method described in the statements below by putting a tick in the relevant column.

Statement	FIFO	LIFO	AVCO
The closing inventory is valued at £6,875.	☐	☐	☐
The issue of 3,750 units is costed at £18,750.	☐	☐	☐
The issue of 3,750 units is costed at £21,875.	☐	☐	☐

2.4 Features of the different methods

FIFO is fairly easy to understand and has the following features:

- In times of rapidly increasing prices, material may be issued at an early and hence unrealistically low price, resulting in the particular job showing an unusually large profit.

- Two jobs started on the same day may show a different cost for the same quantity of the same material.

- In times of rapidly increasing prices FIFO will give a higher profit figure than LIFO or AVCO.

- FIFO can be used in the production of financial statements as it is acceptable to HMRC and International Accounting Standard (IAS) 2 Inventories.

LIFO is also fairly simple to follow and has the following features:

- In contrast to FIFO closing inventories will now be shown at the earliest prices which means that in times of rapidly increasing or decreasing prices, the inventory figure bears little resemblance to the current cost of replacement.

- As with FIFO, two jobs started on the same day may show a different cost for the same quantity of the same material.

- The LIFO method uses the latest prices for issues to production and therefore the cost obtained is more likely to be in line with other costs and selling prices.

- In times of rapidly increasing prices LIFO will give a lower profit figure than FIFO and AVCO.

- LIFO does not adhere to IAS 2 and should not be used for financial reporting of inventory values. LIFO should only be used for internal reporting purposes.

AVCO

- Most suitable when inventory items are so blended it is impossible to assign specific costs to individual units, such as with liquids.

- Is a compromise on valuation of inventory and issues and the average price rarely reflects the actual purchase price of the material.

- Simplifies cost calculations and record keeping

- Can also be used in the production of financial statements as it is acceptable to HMRC and International Accounting Standard (IAS) 2 Inventories.

Test your understanding 4

Identify the correct inventory valuation method from the characteristic given by putting a tick in the relevant column of the table below.

Characteristic	FIFO	LIFO	AVCO
Issues are valued at the most recent purchase cost.	☐	☐	☐
Inventory is valued at the average of the cost of purchases.	☐	☐	☐
Inventory is valued at the most recent purchase cost.	☐	☐	☐

Test your understanding 5

Identify the following statements as either true or false.

Statement	True	False
FIFO costs issues of inventory at the most recent purchase price.	☐	☐
AVCO costs issues of inventory at the oldest purchase price.	☐	☐
LIFO costs issues of inventory at the oldest purchase price.	☐	☐
FIFO values closing inventory at the most recent purchase price.	☐	☐
LIFO values closing inventory at the most recent purchase price.	☐	☐
AVCO values closing inventory at the latest purchase price.	☐	☐

2.5 Impact on profit

The method used to value inventory can have an effect on the profit that is reported by the organisation in any reporting period, as shown in the following example.

 Example 3

Zahra starts a new business as a retailer at the beginning of January, and records the following movements of inventory during the first week of trading:

Date	Purchases			Sales	
	Units	Price/unit	Cost	Units	Price/unit
Jan 3	400	£18.00	£7,200		
Jan 5	200	£21.60	£4,320		
Jan 7				250	£40.00

There was no opening inventory at the start of the week as it is a new business.

The value of closing inventory at the end of the week, using the different valuation methods, is:

- FIFO – £7,020
- LIFO – £6,300
- AVCO – £6,720

(You can check these values for yourself!)

The gross profit shown for each of the three valuation methods is as follows:

	FIFO £	LIFO £	AVCO £
Sales	10,000	10,000	10,000
Cost of sales:			
Opening inventory	0	0	0
Purchases	11,520	11,520	11,520
Closing inventory	(7,020)	(6,300)	(6,720)
	4,500	5,220	4,800
Gross profit	**5,500**	**4,780**	**5,200**

However, whilst each of the three gross profit figures above are different, this is only because of a timing difference. In the long term, the overall profit reported by the organisation will be the same.

To continue with the example, suppose that Zahra buys £7,000 of goods in the following week, and sells all of her inventory for £14,000 (so that, at the end of that week, she has no inventory remaining).

The gross profit shown for week two for each of the three valuation methods would be as follows:

	FIFO £	LIFO £	AVCO £
Sales	14,000	14,000	14,000
Cost of sales:			
Opening inventory	7,020	6,300	6,720
Purchases	7,000	7,000	7,000
Closing inventory	(0)	(0)	(0)
	14,020	13,300	13,720
Gross profit	(20)	700	280

Whilst the profit shown in each individual week depends on the inventory valuation method adopted, the overall profit for the whole period is always the same, at £5,480.

3 Manufacturing accounts

3.1 Basic principles

A manufacturing account shows how the costs of producing the finished goods that are sold during an accounting period has built up. It includes the familiar terms seen so far in your studies, such as direct costs, overheads, WIP and finished goods.

Consider the following extract from the Statement of profit of loss of a manufacturing organisation:

	£
Sales	X
Less cost of goods sold	(X)
	——
Gross profit	X
	——

It can be seen from this that in order to calculate profit an organisation needs to know how much it cost to produce the items it sold. The manufacturing account results in a calculation of the cost of the goods that have been sold. This can then be used in the calculation of profit.

There are five main sections of a manufacturing account:

- direct materials used
- direct cost
- manufacturing cost
- cost of goods manufactured
- cost of goods sold.

We will discuss each section in turn below.

3.2 Direct materials used

The value of direct materials included within the manufacturing account is the direct materials actually **used in production**. This is unlikely to be the same as the cost of the materials that were purchased in the period. This is due to the fact that the organisation may have already had some raw materials in inventory at the beginning of the period, and may also be left with some raw materials at the end of the period as well.

To calculate the value of direct materials we therefore need to adjust for opening and closing inventories of raw materials as follows:

	£
Opening raw materials	X
Plus raw materials purchases in period	X
Less closing raw materials	(X)
	——
Direct materials used	X
	——

Test your understanding 6

A manufacturing organisation has the following cost information for a period:

	£
Purchases of raw materials	25,400
Closing inventory of raw materials	6,500
Opening inventory of raw materials	8,900

Calculate the value of direct materials used.

A   £23,000

B   £25,400

C   £27,800

D   £40,800

3.3   Direct cost

The total value to be included in the direct cost section will include the direct material cost plus any other direct costs. This is therefore likely to include any direct labour cost. There are no inventory adjustments to make for direct labour; it is simply the amount paid.

If we add together the direct materials figure (calculated in the previous section) and the direct labour figure, this gives us a sub-total which is the **direct cost** (or **prime cost**).

Note: you may also see direct expenses being included here as well, although this is less common in manufacturing account questions.

Test your understanding 7

A manufacturing organisation has the following cost information for a period:

	£
Purchases of raw materials	12,000
Direct materials used	18,500
Overheads	6,100
Direct labour	23,300

Calculate the prime cost.

3.4 Manufacturing cost

We have now calculated the direct cost of production. The next stage is to adjust for the indirect costs. These might include indirect materials, indirect labour and any other indirect costs (often termed '**manufacturing overheads**').

The total of all indirect costs is added to the sub-total of direct costs (prime cost) which we have just calculated, to arrive at the **manufacturing cost**.

3.5 Cost of goods manufactured

So far in the calculations we have considered the first stage of the production cycle which was introduced in section 1.1, dealing with the raw materials.

The next stage in the manufacturing process is WIP – where raw materials have started the process of being made into finished goods. At this stage in the manufacturing account we therefore need to adjust the manufacturing cost that we have just calculated for any opening and/or closing WIP, in the same way that we did for our inventories of raw materials:

	£
Manufacturing cost	X
Plus opening WIP	X
Less closing WIP	(X)
Cost of goods manufactured	**X**

Test your understanding 8

A manufacturing organisation has the following costs for a period:

	£
Opening inventory of WIP	15,000
Direct materials used	26,100
Manufacturing overheads	9,000
Direct labour	18,500
Closing inventory of WIP	23,700

Calculate the cost of goods manufactured.

3.6 Cost of goods sold

The final stage of the manufacturing account is to adjust for any inventories of finished goods, to arrive at the cost of goods sold in the period.

The adjustment is the same as we have seen for inventories of raw materials and WIP, as follows:

	£
Cost of goods manufactured	X
Plus opening finished goods	X
Less closing finished goods	(X)
Cost of goods sold	**X**

Test your understanding 9

A manufacturing organisation has the following costs for a period:

	£
Closing inventory of finished goods	50,000
Manufacturing overheads	14,000
Opening inventory of WIP	7,000
Prime cost	38,000
Closing inventory of WIP	9,000
Opening inventory of finished goods	42,000

Calculate the cost of goods sold.

3.7 Complete manufacturing account

If all of the sections above are combined, a full manufacturing account can be produced.

Note the numbers included below are for illustrative purposes only.

Example 4 – Manufacturing account

	£
Opening inventory of raw materials	7,000
Purchases of raw materials	50,000
Closing inventory of raw materials	10,000
DIRECT MATERIALS USED	47,000
Direct labour	97,000
DIRECT COST	**144,000**
Manufacturing overheads	53,000
MANUFACTURING COST	**197,000**
Opening inventory of work in progress	8,000
Closing inventory of work in progress	10,000
COST OF GOODS MANUFACTURED	**195,000**
Opening inventory of finished goods	30,000
Closing inventory of finished goods	25,000
COST OF GOODS SOLD	**200,000**

Test your understanding 10

Which of the following shows the correct order of the sub-totals as they appear in a manufacturing account?

A   Direct cost, cost of goods sold, manufacturing cost, cost of goods manufactured

B   Direct cost, cost of goods manufactured, manufacturing cost, cost of goods sold

C   Direct cost, manufacturing cost, cost of goods sold, cost of goods manufactured

D   Direct cost, manufacturing cost, cost of goods manufactured, cost of goods sold

---

Test your understanding 11

Reorder the following costs into a manufacturing account format:

	£
Manufacturing overheads	47,000
Purchases of raw materials	60,000
MANUFACTURING COST	**147,000**
Opening inventory of raw materials	14,000
Closing inventory of finished goods	70,000
COST OF GOODS SOLD	**147,000**
DIRECT COST	**100,000**
Opening inventory of work in progress	42,000
DIRECT MATERIALS USED	**64,000**
Direct labour	36,000
Closing inventory of raw materials	10,000
Closing inventory of work in progress	32,000
COST OF GOODS MANUFACTURED	**157,000**
Opening inventory of finished goods	60,000

Test your understanding 12

A company has the following cost information for its last accounting period:

	£
Materials costs:	
Direct	50,000
Indirect	12,000
Labour costs:	
Direct	30,000
Indirect	6,000
Factory indirect expenses	82,000

Work in progress and finished goods inventories were as follows:

	£
Work in progress:	
Opening	7,000
Closing	5,000
Finished goods:	
Opening	15,000
Closing	0

Requirement

Complete the table below to show the company's cost structure for the last accounting period:

	£
Prime cost	
Manufacturing overheads	
Total manufacturing costs	
Cost of goods manufactured	
Cost of goods sold	

4 Inventory control

4.1 Introduction

We have already seen that there are three forms that inventory can exist in, being raw materials, work in progress and finished goods.

Most businesses, whatever their size, will be concerned with the problem of which items to have in inventory and how much of each item should be kept.

4.2 Functions of inventory

The principal reasons why a business needs to hold inventory are as follows:

(a) It acts as a buffer in times when there is an unusually high rate of consumption.

(b) It enables the business to take advantage of quantity discounts by buying in bulk.

(c) The business can take advantage of seasonal and other price fluctuations (e.g. buying coal in the summer when it is cheaper).

(d) To prevent any delay in production caused by a lack of raw material so production processes will flow smoothly and efficiently (stock-out).

(e) It may be necessary to hold inventory for a technical reason, for example, whisky must be matured.

4.3 Costs of having inventory

Holding inventory costs money and the principal 'trade-off' in an inventory holding situation is between the costs of acquiring and storing inventories on the one hand and the level of service that the company wishes to provide on the other.

The **total cost of having inventory** consists of the following:

(a) **Purchase price**

(b) **Holding costs**

  – the opportunity cost of capital tied up

  – insurance and security

  – deterioration

  – obsolescence

- damage and theft pilferage

- warehouse upkeep

- stores labour and administration costs.

(c) **Ordering costs**

- clerical and administrative expenses

- transport costs.

(d) **Stock-out costs** (items of required inventory are not available)

- loss of sales, therefore lost contribution

- long-term damage to the business through loss of customer goodwill

- production stoppages caused by a shortage of raw materials

- extra costs caused by the need for emergency orders.

(e) **Inventory recording systems costs**

- maintaining the stores record card.

4.4 Disadvantages of low inventory levels

To keep the holding costs low it may be possible to reduce the volume of inventory that is kept but this can cause some problems:

- Customer demand cannot always be satisfied; this may lead to loss of business if customers become dissatisfied.

- In order to fulfil commitments to important customers, costly emergency procedures (e.g. special production runs) may become necessary in an attempt to maintain customer goodwill.

- It will be necessary to place replenishment orders more frequently than if higher inventories were held, in order to maintain a reasonable service. This will result in higher ordering costs being incurred.

4.5 Disadvantages of high inventory levels

To reduce the problems mentioned above management may consider holding high levels of inventory but again this can have issues:

- Storage or holding costs are very high; such costs will usually include rates, rent, labour, heating, deterioration, etc.

- The cost of the capital tied up in inventories, i.e. the cash spent to buy the inventory, is not available to pay other bills.

- If the stored product becomes obsolete, a large inventory holding of that item could, at worst, represent a large capital investment in an unsaleable product whose cash value is only that of scrap.

- If a great deal of capital is invested in inventories, there will be proportionately less money available for other requirements such as improvement of existing production facilities, or the introduction of new products.

- If there is a sudden drop in the price of a raw material after a high level of inventory has already been purchased, then more has been spent than necessary through purchasing in advance. It follows that it would therefore seem sensible to hold higher inventories during an inflationary period (when prices are rising) and lower inventories during a period of deflation (when prices are falling).

4.6 Inventory control

Inventory control is the method of ensuring that the right **quantity** of the right **quality** of the relevant inventory is available at the right **time** and right **place**.

Inventory control is maintained through the use of inventory record cards and by carrying out inventory checks on a regular basis.

There are two main types of inventory control systems:

(a) fixed quantity system

In a **fixed order system**, a replenishment order of a fixed size is placed when the inventory level falls to a fixed reorder level. Thus a **fixed quantity** is ordered at **variable intervals of time**. This is the most common system used.

(b) periodic (cyclical) review system

In a **periodic review system**, the inventory levels are reviewed at fixed points in time, when the quantity to be ordered is decided. By this method **variable quantities** are ordered at **fixed time intervals**.

Although this may increase the chances of a stock-out (between review times), it has the advantage of being easier to plan the scheduling of inventory counts and orders in advance.

4.7 Inventory control methods

Many inventory control systems will incorporate some or all of the following inventory control levels that assist in keeping costs of inventory holding and ordering down, whilst minimising the chances of stock-outs. The control methods are:

- **buffer inventory** - is the **minimum level** of inventory to be held. It is used to reduce the occurrence of running out of inventory.

- **reorder level** - is the level of inventory that, when reached, an order must be placed to make sure it will be delivered before it runs out.

- **reorder quantity** – this is the amount that will be ordered.

- **Economic order quantity (EOQ)** – is the optimum (most economic) order quantity. It is calculated based on the cost of holding inventory and the cost of ordering inventory:

  (a) the larger the reorder quantity, the higher the inventory levels will be throughout the year therefore the higher the costs of holding

  (b) the larger the reorder quantity, the longer it will take for inventories to fall to the reorder level, therefore the lower the cost of ordering

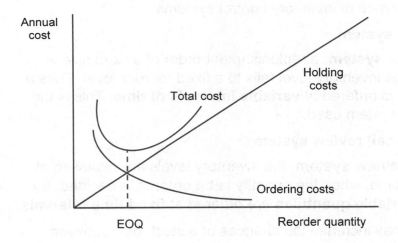

Buffer inventory is also called safety stock.

Test your understanding 13

Identify whether the following statements are true or false.

Statement	True	False
Buffer inventory is the maximum level of inventory that should be held.	☐	☐
Increasing buffer inventory will help reduce storage costs.	☐	☐
Increasing buffer inventory minimises the chances of stock-outs.	☐	☐
In times of changing prices, increasing buffer inventory will help stabilise the cost of inventory held.	☐	☐

Test your understanding 14

A company is trying to decide whether to have a large or small reorder quantity in its inventory control policy.

Identify whether the following statements are true or false.

Statement	True	False
A larger reorder quantity is likely to result in the need for less frequent orders being placed.	☐	☐
A larger reorder quantity is likely to result in lower ordering costs.	☐	☐
A smaller reorder quantity is more likely to lead to lower holding costs.	☐	☐

Test your understanding 15

Identify whether the following statements are true or false.

Statement	True	False
As order quantity rises, average inventory rises.	☐	☐
As order quantity rises, the number of orders rides.	☐	☐
The EOQ is the order quantity which minimises the total costs associated with holding and ordering inventory.	☐	☐

5 Summary

Valuing issues of raw materials and valuing closing inventories are two of the most important techniques that you need to know about in the topic of materials. We have looked at three main methods of pricing issues and valuing inventories in this chapter: FIFO, LIFO, and Weighted Average Cost (AVCO). A common examination task is to ask you to record receipts and issues of materials onto a stores ledger card using one of these methods and value closing inventory.

You also need an understanding of the different costs included in a manufacturing account and to be able to construct such an account in order to calculate the cost of products in manufacturing organisations. An examination question might also require the use of spreadsheet functions to create a manufacturing account. This will be covered in a later chapter.

Another important part of the topic of materials is that of inventory control policies – these assist in keeping the costs of inventory holding and inventory ordering at a minimum, whilst minimising stock-outs at the same time. You need to be able to report on such policies, including buffer stocks and reorder quantities and timings.

6   Further Test your understanding exercises

✎ Test your understanding 16

Identify the correct inventory valuation method from the characteristic given by putting a tick in the relevant column of the table below.

Characteristic	FIFO	LIFO	AVCO
Issues are valued at the most recent purchase cost.	☐	☐	☐
Issues are valued at the oldest purchase cost.	☐	☐	☐
Issues are valued at the average of the cost of purchases.	☐	☐	☐
Inventory is valued at the most recent purchase cost.	☐	☐	☐
Inventory is valued at the oldest purchase cost.	☐	☐	☐

KAPLAN PUBLISHING

Test your understanding 17

Adamkus Ltd has the following movements in a certain inventory item into and out of it stores for the month of March:

Date	Receipts		Issues	
	Units	Cost	Units	Cost
March 5	100	£200		
March 12	100	£250		
March 19	200	£600		
March 23			300	
March 27	400	£1,350		

Complete the table below for the issue and closing inventory values.

Method	Cost of issue on 23 March	Closing inventory at 31 March
FIFO		
LIFO		
AVCO		

Test your understanding 18

Identify the following statements as either true or false.

Statement	True	False
FIFO costs issues of inventory at the oldest purchase price.	☐	☐
AVCO values closing inventory at the oldest purchase price.	☐	☐
LIFO costs issues of inventory at the oldest purchase price.	☐	☐

Test your understanding 19

Reorder the following costs into a manufacturing account format:

	£
COST OF GOODS MANUFACTURED	**31,400**
MANUFACTURING COST	**29,400**
DIRECT COST	**20,000**
COST OF GOODS SOLD	**29,400**
DIRECT MATERIALS USED	12,800
Manufacturing overheads	9,400
Purchases of raw materials	12,000
Opening inventory of raw materials	2,800
Closing inventory of finished goods	14,000
Opening inventory of work in progress	8,400
Direct labour	7,200
Closing inventory of raw materials	2,000
Closing inventory of work in progress	6,400
Opening inventory of finished goods	12,000

Test your understanding 20

The inventory record below shows its raw material receipts and issues to production of product MD2 in June.

Date	Receipts		Issues	
	Kgs	Cost	Kgs	Cost
June 3	1,000	£2,500		
June 15	1,200	£3,330		
June 29			1,400	

(a) Calculate the value of the issue on June 29 assuming that the company uses the AVCO method of inventory valuation.

The direct materials issued above is the direct cost for the production of 500 units of the MD2.

(b) Complete the cost card below to show the total cost and cost per unit of the MD2 for the production of 500 units and also how this would change if production had only been 400 units.

MD2 units produced and sold	500 units	400 units
	£	£
Variable costs:		
Direct materials (see above)		
Direct labour	12,000	
Fixed costs:		
Manufacturing overheads	5,400	
Total cost		
Cost per unit		

Test your understanding answers

 Test your understanding 1

Method	Cost of issue on 19 June	Closing inventory at 30 June
FIFO	£2,000	£3,100
LIFO	£2,200	£2,900
AVCO	£2,080	£3,020

Workings:

FIFO

- The issue will be made up of all 100 units from June 2, all 200 units from June 3 and 100 of those purchased on June 6 at a price of 1,200/200 = £6 per unit

- Cost of issue = £400 + £1,000 + (100 × £6) = £2,000

- Total purchases = £400 + £1,000 + £1,200 + £2,500 = £5,100

- Closing inventory = £5,100 − £2,000 = £3,100

LIFO

- The issue will be made up of all 200 units from June 6 and all 200 units from June 3

- Cost of issue = £1,200 + £1,000 = £2,200

- Closing inventory = £5,100 − £2,200 = £2,900

AVCO

- Before June 19 we had bought a total of 500 units at a total cost of £400 + £1,000 + £1,200 = £2,600

- On average this works out at £2,600/500 = £5.20 per unit

- Thus the cost of the issue will be 400 × £5.20 = £2,080

- Closing inventory = £5,100 − £2,080 = £3,020

Test your understanding 2

Statement	True	False
FIFO values the closing inventory at £1,400.	☐	☑
LIFO costs the issue at £6,100.	☑	☐
AVCO costs the issue at £5,400.	☑	☐

Test your understanding 3

Statement	FIFO	LIFO	AVCO
The closing inventory is valued at £6,875.	☐	☐	☑
The issue of 3,750 units is costed at £18,750.	☑	☐	☐
The issue of 3,750 units is costed at £21,875.	☐	☑	☐

Test your understanding 4

Characteristic	FIFO	LIFO	AVCO
Issues are valued at the most recent purchase cost.	☐	☑	☐
Inventory is valued at the average of the cost of purchases.	☐	☐	☑
Inventory is valued at the most recent purchase cost.	☑	☐	☐

Test your understanding 5

Statement	True	False
FIFO costs issues of inventory at the most recent purchase price.	☐	☑
AVCO costs issues of inventory at the oldest purchase price.	☐	☑
LIFO costs issues of inventory at the oldest purchase price.	☐	☑
FIFO values closing inventory at the most recent purchase price.	☑	☐
LIFO values closing inventory at the most recent purchase price.	☐	☑
AVCO values closing inventory at the latest purchase price.	☐	☑

Test your understanding 6

C	£
Opening inventory of raw materials	8,900
Add purchases of raw materials	25,400
Less closing inventory of raw materials	(6,500)
Direct materials used	**27,800**

Test your understanding 7

Prime cost = direct materials + direct labour + direct expenses
= £18,500 + £23,300
= £41,800

Test your understanding 8

	£
Direct materials used	26,100
Direct labour	18,500
Direct cost	**44,600**
Manufacturing overheads	9,000
Manufacturing cost	**53,600**
Opening WIP	15,000
Closing WIP	(23,700)
Cost of goods manufactured	**44,900**

Test your understanding 9

	£
Direct cost	**38,000**
Manufacturing overheads	14,000
Manufacturing cost	**52,000**
Opening WIP	7,000
Closing WIP	(9,000)
Cost of goods manufactured	**50,000**
Opening finished goods	42,000
Closing finished goods	(50,000)
Cost of goods sold	**42,000**

Test your understanding 10

D Direct cost, manufacturing cost, cost of goods manufactured, cost of goods sold

Test your understanding 11

	£
Opening inventory of raw materials	14,000
Purchases of raw materials	60,000
Closing inventory of raw materials	10,000
DIRECT MATERIALS USED	64,000
Direct labour	36,000
DIRECT COST	**100,000**
Manufacturing overheads	47,000
MANUFACTURING COST	**147,000**
Opening inventory of work in progress	42,000
Closing inventory of work in progress	32,000
COST OF GOODS MANUFACTURED	**157,000**
Opening inventory of finished goods	60,000
Closing inventory of finished goods	70,000
COST OF GOODS SOLD	**147,000**

Test your understanding 12

	£
Prime cost	80,000
Manufacturing overheads	100,000
Total manufacturing costs	180,000
Cost of goods manufactured	182,000
Cost of goods sold	197,000

Prime cost = direct materials + direct labour

= £50,000 + £30,000

Manufacturing overheads = factory indirect expenses + indirect costs

= £82,000 + £12,000 + £6,000

Total manufacturing costs = prime cost + manufacturing overheads

= £80,000 + £100,000

Cost of good manufactured = manufacturing costs + opening WIP - closing WIP

= £180,000 + £7,000 - £5,000

Cost of goods sold = cost of goods manufactured + opening finished goods – closing finished goods

= £182,000 + £15,000 - £0

Test your understanding 13

Statement	True	False
Buffer inventory is the maximum level of inventory that should be held.	☐	☑
Increasing buffer inventory will help reduce storage costs.	☐	☑
Increasing buffer inventory minimises the changes of stock-outs.	☑	☐
In times of changing prices, increasing buffer inventory will help stabilise the cost of inventory held.	☑	☐

Test your understanding 14

Statement	True	False
A larger reorder quantity is likely to result in the need for less frequent orders being placed.	☑	☐
A larger reorder quantity is likely to result in lower ordering costs.	☑	☐
A smaller reorder quantity is more likely to lead to lower holding costs.	☑	☐

Test your understanding 15

Statement	True	False
As order quantity rises, average inventory rises.	☑	☐
As order quantity rises, the number of orders rides.	☐	☑
The EOQ is the order quantity which minimises the total costs associated with holding and ordering inventory.	☑	☐

Test your understanding 16

Characteristic	FIFO	LIFO	AVCO
Issues are valued at the most recent purchase cost.	☐	☑	☐
Issues are valued at the oldest purchase cost.	☑	☐	☐
Issues are valued at the average of the cost of purchases.	☐	☐	☑
Inventory is valued at the most recent purchase cost.	☑	☐	☐
Inventory is valued at the oldest purchase cost.	☐	☑	☐

Test your understanding 17

Method	Cost of issue on 23 March	Closing inventory at 31 March
FIFO	£750	£1,650
LIFO	£850	£1,550
AVCO	£787.50	£1,612.50

Workings:

FIFO

- The issue will be made up of all 100 units from March 5, all 100 units from March 12 and 100 of those purchased on March 19 at a price of £600/200 = £3 per unit

- Cost of issue = £200 + £250 + (100 × £3) = £750

- Total purchases = £200 + £250 + £600 + £1,350 = £2,400

- Closing stock = £2,400 − £750 = £1,650

LIFO

- The issue will be made up of all 200 units from March 19 and 100 units from March 12 at a price of £250/100 = £2.50 per unit

- Cost of issue = £600 + (100 × £2.50) = £850

- Closing stock = £2,400 − £850 = £1,550

AVCO

- Before March 23 we had bought a total of 400 units at a total cost of 200 + 250 + 600 = £1,050

- On average this works out at £1,050/400 = £2.625 per unit

- Thus the cost of the issue will be 300 × £2.625 = £787.50

- Closing stock = £2,400 − £787.5 = £1,612.50

Test your understanding 18

Statement	True	False
FIFO costs issues of inventory at the oldest purchase price.	☑	☐
AVCO values closing inventory at the oldest purchase price.	☐	☑
LIFO costs issues of inventory at the oldest purchase price.	☐	☑

Test your understanding 19

	£
Opening inventory of raw materials	2,800
Purchases of raw materials	12,000
Closing inventory of raw materials	2,000
DIRECT MATERIALS USED	12,800
Direct labour	7,200
DIRECT COST	**20,000**
Manufacturing overheads	9,400
MANUFACTURING COST	**29,400**
Opening inventory of work in progress	8,400
Closing inventory of work in progress	6,400
COST OF GOODS MANUFACTURED	**31,400**
Opening inventory of finished goods	12,000
Closing inventory of finished goods	14,000
COST OF GOODS SOLD	**29,400**

✳ Test your understanding 20

(a)

Date	Receipts		Issues	
	Kgs	Cost	Kgs	Cost
June 3	1,000	£2,500		
June 15	1,200	£3,330		
June 29			1,400	3,710

ACVO means that the issue will be made at the average cost per kg

$$\text{Average cost per kg} = \frac{£2,500 + £3,330}{1,000 \text{ kg} + 1,200 \text{ kg}} = £2.65$$

Cost of issue = 1,400 kg × £2.65 = £3,710.

(b)

MD2 units produced and sold	500 units	400 units
	£	£
Variable costs:		
Direct materials (W1)	3,710	2,968
Direct labour (W2)	12,000	9,600
Fixed costs:		
Manufacturing overheads (W3)	5,400	5,400
Total cost (W4)	21,110	17,968
Cost per unit (W5)	42.22	44.92

(W1) The direct material cost for 500 units is £3,710 (from part (a)).

The direct material cost per unit of MD2 must be £3,710/ 500 = £7.42 per unit.

For 400 units the direct material cost will be £7.42 × 400 = £2,968.

(W2) The direct labour cost for 500 units is given as £12,000.

The direct labour cost per unit of MD2 must be £12,000/ 500 = £24 per unit.

For 400 units the direct labour cost will be £24 × 400 = £9,600.

(W3) The fixed costs will not change with changes in activity level.

(W4) The total cost is the sum of the direct materials, direct labour and manufacturing overheads.

(W5) The cost per unit is the total cost divided by the number of units. For output of 500 units this will be £21,110/ 500 units = £42.22.

Labour costs

Introduction

In this chapter we continue to learn how to establish the unit cost of a product or service, focussing here on the cost of labour. This chapter shows how organisations use a range of techniques to calculate labour payments, including time-rate, overtime, piecework, bonuses and guaranteed minimum payments.

ASSESSMENT CRITERIA	CONTENTS
Costing techniques used in organisations (1.2)	1 Introduction
Calculate labour payments (2.2)	2 Time related pay
Calculate the costs of a product (2.5)	3 Output related pay
	4 Bonus schemes
	5 Sources of information

1 Introduction

1.1 Labour costs

In this unit you need to understand and be able to explain methods of payment for labour to include basic rate (time rate), payment of overtime, payment of bonuses, payment by piecework and guaranteed minimum payments.

You will not be required to have knowledge of specific bonus schemes.

1.2 Direct and indirect labour

Just as materials can be classified as direct or indirect so too can labour costs, depending on the job of the employee.

Example 1

In a manufacturing organisation the factory workers who make the products would be classified as direct labour, whereas the factory supervisor would be an example of an indirect labour cost. Although the supervisor works in the factory, they are not actually making any of the products and so their time cannot be traced directly to each cost unit.

Test your understanding 1

Identify the following statements as true or false by putting a tick in the relevant column of the table below.

Cost	True	False
Direct labour costs can be identified with the goods being made or the service being produced.	☐	☐
Indirect costs vary directly with the level of activity.	☐	☐

1.3 Calculating gross pay

There are two main methods of calculating the gross pay of employees:

- pay employees for the time spent at work (time related pay)
- pay employees for the work actually produced (output related pay).

In addition there may be bonus schemes to be incorporated. These are covered in more detail later in the chapter.

2 Time related pay

2.1 Time related pay

Employees paid under a time related pay method are paid for the hours that they spend at work, regardless of the amount of production or output that they achieve in that time. Time related pay employees can be split into two types, **salaried employees** and **hourly rate employees**.

2.2 Salaried employees

 Definition

A **salaried employee** is one whose gross pay is agreed at a fixed amount for a period of time whatever hours that employee works in that period.

Annual salaries tend to be paid to management and non-production staff such as administrators, secretaries, accounts staff etc.

This might be expressed as an annual salary such as £19,500 per year or as a weekly or monthly rate such as £325 per week or £1,625 per month.

Each organisation will have a set number of hours that are expected to be worked each week, for example a standard working week of 37.5 hours, and salaried employees will be expected to work for at least this number of hours each week.

However, if the salaried employee works for more than the standard number of hours for the week then the employment agreement may specify that overtime payments are to be made for the additional hours.

2.3 Hourly rate employees

 Definition

An **hourly rate employee** is one who is paid a set hourly rate for each hour that they work.

Many production and manual workers will be paid for every hour that they work. These employees are paid for the actual number of hours of attendance in a period, usually a week. A rate of pay will be set for each hour of attendance. In general, hourly paid workers will have a standard number of hours that they work each week. If they work for more than this number of hours then they are said to have worked **overtime**, which is usually paid at more than the basic hourly rate.

2.4 Overtime and overtime premium

 Definition

Overtime is the number of hours worked by an employee which is greater than the number of hours set by the organisation as the standard working week.

 Definition

Overtime premium is the amount **over and above** the normal hourly rate that employees are paid for overtime hours.

It is common that employees who work overtime are paid an additional amount per hour for those extra hours, for example, time and a half or double time.

Overtime has two terms that you need to be aware of – overtime payment and overtime premium.

- The **overtime payment** is the **total** amount paid for hours worked above the normal number of hours.

- The **overtime premium** is the **extra** paid above the normal rate for those overtime hours. For example, if an employee is paid time and a half for any hours above his/her basic, then the 'half' is the premium.

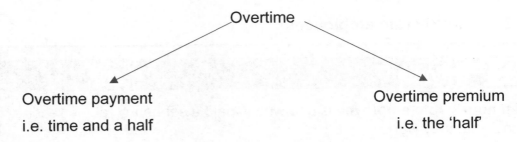

This distinction is often necessary for costing purposes, as the premium part of the overtime may be classified separately from the overtime hours at basic rate.

 Example 2

An employee's basic week is 40 hours at a rate of pay of £8 per hour. Overtime is paid at 'time and a half'. The employee works a 45-hour week. What is the total gross pay for this employee for the week?

	£
Basic hours (40 hrs × £8)	320.00
Overtime (5 hrs × £8 × 1.5)	60.00
	————
	380.00
	————

The overtime payment can be split between the basic rate element and the overtime premium:

	£
Basic pay (5 hrs × £8)	40.00
Overtime premium (5 hrs × £4)	20.00
	————
	60.00
	————

 Test your understanding 2

Singh Ltd pays a time-rate of £12 per hour to its direct labour for a standard 35 hour week. Any of the labour force working in excess of 35 hours is paid an overtime rate of £15 per hour.

Calculate the gross wage for the week for the workers in the table below.

Worker	Hours worked	Basic wage £	Overtime £	Gross wage £
J. Patel	35			
D. Smith	38			
S. O'Leary	42			

Test your understanding 3

Cashier Ltd pays a time-rate of £15 per hour to its direct labour for a standard 35 hour week. Any of the workforce working in excess of 35 hours per week is paid an overtime rate of time and a half.

Calculate the gross wage for the week for the workers in the table below.

Worker	Hours worked	Basic wage £	Overtime premium £	Gross wage £
S. Lawton	41			
M. Singh	36			

Test your understanding 4

Identify the labour payment method by putting a tick in the relevant column of the table below.

Payment method	Overtime	Overtime premium	Hourly	Salaried
Labour is paid based on the number of hours worked.	☐	☐	☐	☐
Labour is paid at a fixed amount for a set period.	☐	☐	☐	☐
The extra amount paid above the normal hourly rate.	☐	☐	☐	☐
The total amount paid for hours worked above normal hours.	☐	☐	☐	☐

3 Output related pay

3.1 Introduction

Output related pay is also known as 'payment by results' or 'piecework'. This is a direct alternative to time related pay.

Definition

Payment by results or piecework is where a fixed amount is paid per unit of output achieved irrespective of the time spent.

3.2 Advantages of payment by results

- It produces a constant labour cost per unit.

- It **encourages efficient work** – the harder an employee works and the more units they produce, the higher the wage they will earn (within certain parameters).

3.3 Problems with payment by results

- Employees **lack security of income**, so may become demotivated. (This can be addressed through guarantees, see next section).

- The employee can be **penalised** for low levels of production due to factors that are outside his/her control (e.g. machine breakdowns).

- Maintaining **quality of the output** produced. If the employee is paid by the amount that is produced then the temptation might be to produce more units but of a lower quality.

- An accurate system of job sheets and checking of job sheets needs to be in place to ensure accurate recording of actual output produced, to avoid instances of abuse to the system.

For these reasons, basic piecework systems are rare in practice – variations of these systems are used instead.

Test your understanding 5

Stizgt Ltd uses a piecework method to pay labour in one of its factories. The rate used is 90p per unit produced.

Calculate the gross wage for the week for the workers in the table below.

Worker	Units produced in week	Gross wage £
S. McHenry	200 units	
D. Weaver	320 units	
S. Hasina	250 units	

3.4 Piece rate with guarantee

A **piece rate with guarantee** gives the employee some security if the employer does not provide enough work in a particular period. The way that the system works is that if an employee's earnings for the amount of units produced in the period are lower than the guaranteed amount then the guaranteed amount is paid instead.

Test your understanding 6

Fernando is paid £3.00 for every unit that he produces but he has a guaranteed wage of £28.00 per eight hour day. In a particular week he produces the following number of units:

Monday	12 units
Tuesday	14 units
Wednesday	9 units
Thursday	14 units
Friday	8 units

Calculate Fernando's wage for this week.

Test your understanding 7

Venus Ltd pays £14 per hour to its direct labour force for a standard 35 hour week. Any employees working for more than the standard hours will be paid overtime, at time and a half.

Venus Ltd is considering introducing a piecework scheme and paying £8 per completed unit instead.

Complete the table below for the two employees. Enter a zero where applicable.

Worker	Hours worked	Basic wage £	Overtime premium £	Gross wages £	Units	Piece-work wages £
A. Wolf	35				65	
K. Oveja	41				75	

4 Bonus schemes

4.1 Basic principle of bonuses

Bonuses may be paid to employees for a variety of reasons. An individual employee, a department, a division or the entire organisation may have performed particularly well and it is felt by the management that a bonus is due to some or all of the employees.

The basic principle of a bonus payment is that the employee is rewarded for any additional income or savings in cost to the organisation. This may be, for example, because the employee has managed to save a certain amount of time on the production of a product or a number of products. This time saving will save the organisation money and the amount saved will tend to be split between the organisation and the employee on some agreed basis. The amount paid to the employee/employees is known as the bonus.

The typical bonus payable will often depend on the method of payment of the employee. The calculation and payment of bonuses will differ for salaried employees, employees paid by results and employees paid on a time rate basis.

4.2 Individual bonuses

Bonus schemes are a compromise between a day rate and a piecework system. Earnings will comprise:

(a) a day rate amount, based on hours worked, and

(b) a bonus based on quantity produced (usually above a certain standard) or on time saved in relation to standard time allowance for the output achieved.

Example 3

On a particular day, Faith worked for 7.5 hours, producing 20 units. The standard time allowance for each unit is 30 minutes. Faith's basic hourly rate is £9.00 and she is paid a bonus for time saved from standard at 50% of her basic hourly rate.

Calculate Faith's pay for the day.

Solution

		£
Day rate = 7.5 hours × £9.00		67.50
Bonus:		
Standard time to produce 20 units (20 units × 30 mins)	10 hours	
Actual time taken	7.5 hours	
	————	
Time saved	2.5 hours	
	————	
Bonus = 2.5 hrs × £9.00 × 50%		11.25
		————
Total		78.75
		————

Test your understanding 8

Meidani Ltd uses a time-rate method with bonus to pay its direct labour in one of its factories. The time-rate used is £10 per hour and a worker is expected to produce 6 units an hour, anything over this and the worker is paid a bonus of £2 per unit.

Calculate the gross wage for the week for the workers in the table below.

Worker	Hours worked	Units produced	Basic wage £	Bonus £	Gross wage £
J. Klestil	35	220			
C. Zemin	35	205			
J. Chirac	40	240			

4.3 Group bonuses

In the case of, for example, an assembly line, where it is impossible for an individual worker on the line to increase productivity without the others also doing so, a group bonus scheme may be used. The bonus is calculated by reference to the output of the group.

 Example 4

A factory manufacturing chocolate bars employs ten production workers. The standard output for the group is 2,500 bars per day.

A weekly bonus of £30 per employee is paid for each complete percent that actual output exceeds the standard.

Last week's target was 17,500 bars and actual output was 19,250 units.

Calculate the total cost of the bonus paid last week.

Solution

The standard number of units for the time worked:

2,500 bars per day × 7 days = 17,500 bars

The number of excess units produced:

19,250 – 17,500 = 1,750 bars

Percentage:

Excess/standard × 100 = 1,750/17,500 × 100 = 10%

Bonus per employee:

£30 × 10 = £300

Total bonus for 10 employees for the week:

£300 × 10 = £3,000

 Test your understanding 9

A factory manufacturing toy cars pays its assembly workers £15 per hour for a standard 35 hour week. It does not offer any overtime, but instead offers a bonus based on the number of cars manufactured.

In a standard week, employees are expected to manufacture 100 units each. Any units made in excess of this are paid a bonus of £5.00 per unit, to a maximum of 130 units.

There are currently two teams in the assembly department, Team Red and Team Blue, each containing five employees. A group bonus of £150 is available if all five employees exceed their weekly target. This bonus is shared equally amongst team members.

In the previous week, only three members of Team Red exceeded their production target, whereas all five members of Team Blue exceeded the target.

Complete the following table to show the gross weekly wage for one member of each team.

	Hours worked	Units produced	Basic pay £	Individual bonus £	Team bonus £	Gross wage £
Team Red employee	37	136				
Team Blue employee	38	126				

Test your understanding 10

Willow Ltd employs 5 production workers in a factory.

All employees are paid a basic rate of £12 per hour for a standard 35-hour working week (Monday to Friday).

Any overtime during the week is paid at time and a half.

Any overtime at the weekends is paid at double time.

(a) Complete the following table to show the pay for the previous week for each employee.

Hours worked (Mon-Fri)	Hours worked (Week-end)	Basic pay £	Overtime premium (Mon-Fri) £	Overtime premium (Weekend) £	Gross pay £
42	3				

The standard output per employee is 250 units per week. If this is exceeded then each employee is paid a bonus in addition to the hourly wage at a rate of £2 per unit. Last week, each employee produced 275 units.

(b) Calculate the bonus paid to each employee.

(c) Calculate the total pay, including bonuses, for Willow Ltd for last week.

4.4 Bonus cap

We have seen that employees may be paid a bonus where output exceeds a certain level. For example, if output is greater than 350 units in a given week, then a bonus of £0.20 per unit may be applied. This incentivises workers to achieve higher levels of output. However, companies will often place a '**cap**' on the bonus, so that it is only paid up to a certain level of output. Continuing our previous example, the bonus may be capped at 500 units. Therefore, a bonus will be paid for all units produced over 350 units, but not for units produced in excess of 500 units. If an employee was to produce 550 units, for example, then the bonus would only be paid for units 351-500 (and not for units 501-550).

Example 5

A company has a production target of 400 units for each production employee per week. Any excess production is rewarded by a bonus of £6 per unit, capped at a maximum production of 480 units.

An employee who produces 420 units in the week will earn a bonus on the 20 additional units they produce:

Bonus = 20 units × £6 = £120

An employee who produces 500 units in the week will only earn a bonus on the units up to 480. Any units above the bonus cap will not earn a bonus (so units 481 - 500):

Bonus = 80 units × £6 = £480

An employee who produces 400 units will not earn a bonus. The bonus is only paid for any units made **in excess** of 400, and so the first unit to earn a bonus will be unit 401.

 Test your understanding 11

A company has a production target of 350 units for each production employee in a given week. Any excess production is rewarded with a bonus of £7 per unit, capped at a maximum production of 400 units.

Identify whether the bonus calculations for the following employees are correct or incorrect:

Bonus calculation	Correct	Incorrect
Employee 1 produces 340 units and earns a bonus of £0.	☐	☐
Employee 2 produces 350 units and earns a bonus of £7.	☐	☐
Employee 3 produces 370 units and earns a bonus of £140.	☐	☐
Employee 4 produces 420 units and earns a bonus of £490.	☐	☐

Test your understanding 12

Identify the labour payment method by putting a tick in the relevant column of the table below.

Payment method	Time-rate	Piece-rate	Time-rate plus bonus
Labour is paid based on the production achieved.	☐	☐	☐
Labour is paid according to hours worked with an extra amount added on if an agreed level of output is exceeded.	☐	☐	☐
Labour is paid according to hours worked.	☐	☐	☐

Test your understanding 13

Identify one **advantage** for each labour payment method by putting a tick in the relevant column of the table below.

Payment method	Time-rate	Piece-rate	Time-rate plus bonus
Assured level of remuneration for employee.	☐	☐	☐
Employee earns more if they work more efficiently than expected.	☐	☐	☐
Assured level of remuneration and reward for working efficiently.	☐	☐	☐

5 Sources of information

5.1 Documentation and procedures to record labour costs

When an employee joins an organisation it must record details of the employee, their job and pay. This is done by the HR department in the individual employee's personnel record.

Details that might be kept about an employee are as follows:

- full name, address and date of birth

- personal details such as marital status and emergency contact name and address

- National Insurance number

- previous employment history

- educational details

- professional qualifications

- date of joining organisation

- employee number or code

- clock number issued

- job title and department

- rate of pay agreed

- holiday details agreed

- bank details if salary is to be paid directly into bank account

- amendments to any of the details above (such as increases in agreed rates of pay)

- date of termination of employment (when this takes place) and reasons for leaving.

5.2 Employee record of attendance

On any particular day an employee may be at work, on holiday, absent due to sickness or absent for some other reason. A record must be kept of these details for each day.

This information about an employee's attendance will come from various sources such as clock cards, time sheets, job sheets, and job cards.

6 Summary

This chapter has considered the different methods of calculating the cost of labour within an organisation. These may include time-rate (including overtime), piecework, bonus schemes (individual and group) and guaranteed minimum payments. Make sure you can distinguish between these different techniques and are able to apply the calculations to questions.

7 Further test your understanding exercises

Test your understanding 14

Karimov Ltd pays a time-rate of £10 per hour to its direct labour for a standard 37 hour week. Any of the labour force working in excess of 37 hours is paid 'time and a half'.

Calculate the gross wage for the week for the workers in the table below.

Worker	Hours worked	Basic wage £	Overtime premium £	Gross wage £
M. Khan	42			
D. Murphy	37			
K. Ng	40			

Test your understanding 15

Motor Ltd is a car manufacturer. Classify the following costs by nature (direct or indirect) in the table below.

Cost	Direct	Indirect
Basic pay for production workers	☐	☐
Factory supervisors wages	☐	☐
Accountant's salary	☐	☐
Production workers overtime premium	☐	☐
Factory cleaner's wages	☐	☐

KAPLAN PUBLISHING

Test your understanding 16

All production workers in a factory are paid as follows:

- For a basic five-hour shift every day from Monday to Friday – basic pay of £12 per hour.

- For any overtime in excess of the basic five hours, on any day from Monday to Friday – the extra hours are paid at time-and-a-half.

- For two contracted hours each Saturday morning – basic pay.

- For any hours in excess of two hours on Saturday – the extra hours are paid at double time.

- For any hours worked on Sunday – paid at double time.

The table below shows the daily hours worked last week for employee Sian Mentez. Complete the columns, entering zero figures in cells where appropriate.

	Hours	Basic pay £	Overtime premium £	Gross pay £
Monday	5			
Tuesday	9			
Wednesday	5			
Thursday	5			
Friday	8			
Saturday	5			
Sunday	2			
Total				

Test your understanding 17

The following information relates to the total direct labour costs incurred during March 20X9:

Normal time hours worked	2,000 hours
Overtime at time and a half worked	400 hours
Overtime at double time worked	150 hours
Total hours worked	2,550 hours
Normal time hourly rate	£9 per hour

Overtime premiums paid are included as part of direct labour costs.

The total cost of direct labour for the month of March 20X9 is:

A   £21,150

B   £22,950

C   £26,100

D   £31,050

 Test your understanding 18

Gibson plc uses a piecework method to pay labour to make clothing in one of its factories. The rate used is £2.50 per garment completed.

Calculate the gross wage for the week for the workers in the table below. (Calculations to two d.p.)

Worker	Units produced in week	Gross wage £
H. Potter	100 units	
T. Riddle	130 units	
S. Snape	175 units	

Test your understanding 19

Leona is paid £5.00 for every unit that she produces but she has a guaranteed minimum wage of £25.00 per day.

Calculate Leona's wage for this week by filling in the following table:

Day	Units produced	Gross wage £
Monday	4 units	
Tuesday	6 units	
Wednesday	9 units	
Thursday	3 units	
Friday	8 units	
Total	30 units	

 Test your understanding 20

Legolas Ltd uses a time-rate method with bonus to pay its direct labour in one of its factories. The time-rate used is £12 per hour and a worker is expected to produce 10 units an hour, anything over this and the worker is paid a bonus of £1 per unit.

Calculate the gross wage for the week for the workers in the table below.

Worker	Hours worked	Units produced	Basic wage £	Bonus £	Gross wage £
L. Aragon	37	375			
T. Ent	35	360			
K. Theodin	42	410			

Test your understanding answers

Test your understanding 1

Cost	True	False
Direct labour costs can be identified with the goods being made or the service being produced.	☑	☐
Indirect costs vary directly with the level of activity.	☐	☑

Test your understanding 2

Worker	Hours worked	Basic wage £	Overtime £	Gross wage £
J. Patel	35	420	0	420
D. Smith	38	420	45	465
S. O'Leary	42	420	105	525

Test your understanding 3

Worker	Hours worked	Basic wage £	Overtime premium £	Gross wage £
S. Lawton	41	615	45	660
M. Singh	36	540	7.50	547.50

Test your understanding 4

Payment method	Overtime	Overtime premium	Hourly	Salaried
Labour is paid based on the number of hours worked.	☐	☐	☑	☐
Labour is paid at a fixed amount for a set period.	☐	☐	☐	☑
The extra amount paid above the normal hourly rate.	☐	☑	☐	☐
The total amount paid for hours worked above normal hours.	☑	☐	☐	☐

Test your understanding 5

Worker	Units produced in week	Gross wage £
S. McHenry	200 units	180.00
D. Weaver	320 units	288.00
S. Hasina	250 units	225.00

Test your understanding 6

Fernando would be paid £176.

Working

Total weekly wage

	£
Monday (12 × 3)	36
Tuesday (14 × 3)	42
Wednesday (guarantee)	28
Thursday (14 × 3)	42
Friday (guarantee)	28
	176

The payment of a guaranteed amount is not a bonus for good work but simply an additional payment required if the amount of production is below a certain level.

 Test your understanding 7

Worker	Hours worked	Basic wage £	Overtime premium £	Gross wages £	Units	Piece-work wages £
A. Wolf	35	490	0	490	65	520
K. Oveja	41	574	42	616	75	600

Workings

- A. Wolf: 35 hours × £14 = £490, no overtime.
  65 units produced × £8 per unit = £520.

- K. Oveja: 41 hours × £14 = £574 plus overtime premium @ 6 hours × £7 = £42.
  75 units produced × £8 per unit = £600.

KAPLAN PUBLISHING

Test your understanding 8

Worker	Hours worked	Units produced	Basic wage £	Bonus £	Gross wage £
J. Klestil	35	220	350	20	370
C. Zemin	35	205	350	0	350
J. Chirac	40	240	400	0	400

Working

- Basic wage = £10 × hours worked.

- In 35 hours we would expect 35 × 6 = 210 units.
  J Klestil exceeded this by 10 units, giving a bonus of 10 × 2 = £20.
  C. Zemin did not, so received no bonus.

- In 40 hours we would expect 40 × 6 = 240 units.
  J. Chirac did not exceed this, so received no bonus.

Test your understanding 9

	Hours worked	Units produced	Basic pay £	Individual bonus £	Team bonus £	Gross wage £
Team Red employee	37	136	555	150	0	705
Team Blue employee	38	126	570	130	30	730

Team Red employee:

Basic wage = 37 hours × £15 per hour = £555

Individual bonus = (130 − 100) × £5 = £150

(Note – remember the bonus is capped at 130 units)

Team bonus = nil, as only three of the five team members exceeded the required target

Gross wage = £555 + £150 = £705.

Team Blue employee:

Basic wage = 38 hours × £15 per hour = £570

Individual bonus = (126 – 100) × £5 = £130

Team bonus = £150/5 = £30

Gross wage = £570 + £130 + £30 = £730.

 Test your understanding 10

(a)

Hours worked (Mon-Fri)	Hours worked (Week-end)	Basic pay £	Overtime premium (Mon-Fri) £	Overtime premium (Weekend) £	Gross pay £
42	3	540	42	36	618

(b) Excess production per employee = 275 – 250 = 25 units.

Bonus paid at £2 per unit = 25 units × £2 = £50 per employee.

(c) Total pay:

Gross pay (£618 × 5 employees)	£3,090
Bonus (£50 × 5 employees)	£250
	£3,340

Test your understanding 11

Bonus calculation	Correct	Incorrect
Employee 1 produces 340 units and earns a bonus of £0.	☑	☐
Employee 2 produces 350 units and earns a bonus of £7.	☐	☑
Employee 3 produces 370 units and earns a bonus of £140.	☑	☐
Employee 4 produces 420 units and earns a bonus of £490.	☐	☑

Employee 1 has not reached the production target of 350 units and so will not earn a bonus.

Employee 2 has reached the target, but not produced any units in excess of the target. The bonus will be paid for units 351 upwards.

Employee 3 has produced 20 units more than the production target, and so will earn a bonus of 20 × £7 = £140.

Employee 4 has produced 70 units more than the production target. However, the bonus is capped at 400 units, and so the bonus will only be paid on units 351–400 (50 units). The maximum bonus payable will therefore be 50 × £7 = £350.

Test your understanding 12

Payment method	Time-rate	Piece-rate	Time-rate plus bonus
Labour is paid based on the production achieved.	☐	☑	☐
Labour is paid according to hours worked with an extra amount added on if an agreed level of output is exceeded.	☐	☐	☑
Labour is paid according to hours worked.	☑	☐	☐

Test your understanding 13

Payment method	Time-rate	Piece-rate	Time-rate plus bonus
Assured level of remuneration for employee.	☑	☐	☐
Employee earns more if they work more efficiently than expected.	☐	☑	☐
Assured level of remuneration and reward for working efficiently.	☐	☐	☑

Test your understanding 14

Worker	Hours worked	Basic wage £	Overtime premium £	Gross wage £
M. Khan	42	420	25	445
D. Murphy	37	370	0	370
K. Ng	40	400	15	415

Test your understanding 15

Cost	Direct	Indirect
Basic pay for production workers	☑	☐
Factory supervisors wages	☐	☑
Accountant's salary	☐	☑
Production workers overtime premium	☑	☐
Factory cleaner's wages	☐	☑

Test your understanding 16

	Hours	Basic pay £	Overtime premium £	Gross pay £
Monday	5	60	0	60
Tuesday	9	108	24	132
Wednesday	5	60	0	60
Thursday	5	60	0	60
Friday	8	96	18	114
Saturday	5	60	36	96
Sunday	2	24	24	48
Total	39	468	102	570

Test your understanding 17

C

Basic pay 2,550 hrs @ £9	£22,950
Overtime (time and a half) 400 hrs @ £4.50	£1,800
Overtime (double time) 150 hrs @ £9	£1,350
	£26,100

Test your understanding 18

Worker	Units produced in week	Gross wage £
H. Potter	100 units	250.00
T. Riddle	130 units	325.00
S. Snape	175 units	437.50

Test your understanding 19

Day	Units produced	Gross wage £
Monday	4 units	25
Tuesday	6 units	30
Wednesday	9 units	45
Thursday	3 units	25
Friday	8 units	40
Total	30 units	165

Test your understanding 20

Worker	Hours worked	Units produced	Basic wage £	Bonus £	Gross wage £
L. Aragon	37	375	444	5	449
T. Ent	35	360	420	10	430
K. Theodin	42	410	504	0	504

Overheads

5

Introduction

Overhead is a large, and in many cases the largest, component of cost. This chapter looks at how overheads (or indirect costs) are absorbed into the cost of a product or service using **absorption rates**, to establish the unit cost. We will then use this unit cost information, together with the brought forward knowledge on cost behaviour, in the calculation of total and unit costs at different levels of output and for different types of organisations.

ASSESSMENT CRITERIA	CONTENTS
Costing techniques used in organisations (1.2)	1 Overheads
Sources of information on income and expenditure (1.4)	2 Overhead absorption
Calculate overhead absorption rates (2.3)	3 Total and unit costs
Use cost behaviour to calculate total and unit costs (2.4)	4 Other costing systems
Calculate the costs of a product (2.5)	

1 Overheads

1.1 Introduction

Remember in a previous chapter we saw how the total unit cost of product or service is made up of direct costs plus indirect costs, or 'overheads', which can be shown on an example unit cost card as follows:

	£
Direct materials (3kg @ £5 per kg)	15
Direct labour (4 hours @ £10 per hour)	40
Direct expenses	12
Direct cost (or 'prime cost')	**67**
Overheads (indirect costs)	15
Total product unit cost	**82**

Identifying **direct materials and labour** should be straightforward, or the costs would not be classified as 'direct'.

- Direct materials could be identified using job cards and information on stores requisitions (as outlined in chapter 3).

- Direct labour can be identified using job cards and time sheets (as outlined in chapter 4).

Indirect expenses, however, cannot be identified with a specific cost unit.

Depending upon their nature, indirect expenses may be:

- production costs (production overheads); or

- non-production costs (non-production overheads).

Production overheads are included in the total production cost of a product. They could include factory rent, rates, insurance, light, heat, power and other factory running costs. In the following sections we will learn how to identify the overhead costs to be included within the cost unit.

2 Overhead absorption

2.1 Overhead absorption rate

Because it is more difficult to identify overheads with units of output, some system needs to be developed for either averaging overheads over units or absorbing them into units. This is particularly important when a company makes more than one product.

> ### 🔍 Definition
>
> **Overhead absorption** is the charging of a production cost centre's overhead costs to the cost units produced by the cost centre.

The **absorption rate** is calculated at the start of the period and is therefore **based on budgeted activity** and on **budgeted overheads**. Various bases for absorption exist and the most suitable one should be chosen depending on the situation.

This is discussed in more detail in other units in your studies, but here you need to be aware of three approaches:

- Unit basis
- Labour hour basis
- Machine hour basis

2.2 Unit basis

If an organisation only produces one type of product then it is possible to calculate the amount of overhead to absorb into the product cost as follows:

$$\text{Overhead rate per unit} = \frac{\text{Budgeted overheads}}{\text{Budgeted units produced}}$$

This method would be most appropriate in an organisation that **only produces one product.** Each unit absorbs the same amount of overhead.

Example 1

Autumn Ltd produces one product. Each unit of the product uses £20 worth of direct material and £10 of direct labour.

Autumn Ltd has budgeted overheads of £27,000 for the next accounting period and expects to produce 13,500 units.

Calculate the total cost per unit if Autumn Ltd absorbs overheads on a per unit basis.

Solution

Total cost per unit

Materials	£20
Labour	£10
Overheads (working)	£2
	———
	£32
	———

Working

$$\text{Overhead rate} = \frac{\text{Budgeted overheads}}{\text{Budgeted units produced}} = \frac{£27,000}{13,500 \text{ units}} = £2 \text{ per unit}$$

 Test your understanding 1

Staple Ltd produces only one product. It has budgeted overheads of £35,000 for the next accounting period and expects to produce 1,750 units.

Calculate the overhead cost per unit if overheads on a per unit basis.

Test your understanding 2

Wigwam Ltd is costing a single product which has the following cost details

Variable cost per unit

Materials   (5 kg @ £6 per kg)

Labour   (2 hours @ £12 per hour)

Total fixed costs   £80,000

Calculate the unit cost if Wigwam Ltd has budgeted to produce 12,500 units and absorbs overheads on a unit basis.

The use of an absorption rate per unit is appropriate for single-product businesses/cost centres, but **may be inappropriate for multi-product businesses**.

Bases commonly used as an alternative to the rate per unit, when more than one product is involved, are rates per labour hour or per machine hour.

The calculations are the same as we have just seen, but rather than dividing by budgeted units, budgeted activity it used:

$$\text{Overhead rate} = \frac{\text{Budgeted overheads}}{\text{Budgeted activity level}}$$

Whichever method is used, the result will still only be a rough estimate of what each product costs as it is based on budgeted figures.

2.3   Labour hour basis

Here overheads are absorbed as a rate per direct labour hour. This means that for every hour someone works on the unit, an hour's worth of overhead is given to the unit as well.

$$\text{Overhead rate per labour hour} = \frac{\text{Budgeted overhead}}{\text{Budgeted labour hours}}$$

This method would be useful in a business that is **labour intensive**.

Example 2

Sculpture Ltd manufactures many different products. It is currently costing one of its products which has the following cost details:

Variable cost per unit

Materials   (8kg @ £25 per kg)
Labour   (4 hours @ £15 per hour)
Total fixed costs   £75,000

Calculate the unit cost for the above product if Sculpture Ltd has budgeted for 15,000 direct labour hours in the next year and overheads are absorbed using a rate per labour hour basis.

Solution

Total cost per unit

Materials (8kg × £25)	£200
Labour (4 hrs × £15)	£60
Overheads (4 hrs × £5 (working))	£20
	£280

Working

$$\text{Overhead rate} = \frac{\text{Budgeted overheads}}{\text{Budgeted labour hours}} = \frac{£75,000}{15,000 \text{ hours}} = £5 \text{ per hour}$$

 Test your understanding 3

Taupe Ltd is a multi-product organisation. It has budgeted overheads of £147,000 for the next accounting period and expects to produce 17,500 units. Each unit requires 1.5 direct labour hours.

Calculate the overhead cost per unit if overheads are absorbed on a rate per labour hour.

Test your understanding 4

Accent Ltd is a multi-product organisation. Cost details for one of its products are showing below.

Variable cost per unit

Materials	(7 kg @ £5 per kg)
Labour	(0.5 hours @ £30 per hour)
Total fixed costs	£120,000

Calculate the unit cost if Accent Ltd has budgeted for 6,000 labour hours and absorbs overheads using a rate per labour hour basis.

2.4 Machine hour basis

The calculation here is as in 2.3 above, but rather than calculating a labour rate per hour, budgeted machine hours are used to find an overhead rate per machine hour. This means that for every hour a machine is used to make a unit an hour's worth of overhead is given to the unit as well.

$$\text{Overhead rate per machine hour} = \frac{\text{Budgeted overhead}}{\text{Budgeted machine hours}}$$

This would be most appropriate for an organisation that is **machine intensive**.

Example 3

Fatima manufactures a range of wooden furniture. She wants to know the unit cost for one of the tables, which has the following cost details:

Variable cost per unit

Materials	£140
Labour	£75
Total overheads	£40,000

Each table takes 2 hours of machine time to manufacture. Fatima absorbs overheads using a rate per machine hour and expects to use 2,500 machine hours in this period.

Calculate the unit cost for the table.

Solution

Total cost per unit

Materials	£140
Labour	£75
Overheads (2 hours × £16 (working))	£32
	——
	£247
	——

Working

$$\text{Overhead rate} = \frac{\text{Budgeted overheads}}{\text{Budgeted machine hours}} = \frac{\text{£40,000}}{\text{2,500 hours}} = \text{£16 per hour}$$

 Test your understanding 5

Summer Ltd is a multi-product organisation. It has budgeted overheads of £350,000 for the next accounting period and expects to produce 20,000 units. Each unit requires five machine hours.

Calculate the overhead cost per unit if overheads are absorbed on a rate per machine hour.

Test your understanding 6

Spirali Ltd is a multi-product organisation. Cost details for one of its products are showing below:

Variable cost per unit	
Materials	(12 kg @ £4 per kg)
Labour	(3 hours @ £20 per hour)
Machine time	3 hours
Total fixed costs	£90,000

Calculate the unit cost of the product if Spirali Ltd has budgeted for 15,000 machine hours and absorbs overheads using a rate per machine hour.

Test your understanding 7

Mint Ltd is considering how to cost the various products it makes and is deciding on the most appropriate absorption basis.

(a) Complete the table below to show the three overhead absorption rates that Mint Ltd could use. Show your workings to two decimal places.

	Machine hour	Labour hour	Unit
Overheads (£)	200,000	200,000	200,000
Activity	10,000	80,000	8,000
Absorption rate (£)			

(b) One of the products manufactured by Mint Ltd is the Peppermint. Each unit of the Peppermint takes 15 minutes machine time and 30 minutes labour time.

Use each of the three overhead absorption rates calculated in (a) above to calculate the unit cost of the Peppermint. Show your workings to two decimal places.

	Machine hour £	Labour hour £	Unit £
Direct cost	25.00	25.00	25.00
Overheads			
Total unit cost			

(c) Which of the three absorption methods would be most suitable for Mint Ltd?

3 Total and unit costs

3.1 Introduction

We have now seen how the total cost of a product is made up of several elements and are able to value each of those elements.

This information, together with the knowledge of cost behaviour, can then be used in order to calculate the total or unit costs at different levels of output. This is especially useful for budgeting purposes.

3.2 Total cost

If we were classifying costs by nature, we would say that:

Total cost = direct costs + indirect costs (overheads)

Similarly, if we were classifying costs by behaviour, we would say that:

Total cost = fixed costs + variable costs

The key to calculating total and units costs is remembering how different costs behave.

3.3 Variable costs

Remember that:

- Total variable costs vary depending on the output level:

    Total variable cost = (variable cost per unit × output level)

- Where the variable cost per unit is not known, we can rearrange the above formula to find that

    $$\text{Variable cost per unit} = \frac{\text{Total variable cost}}{\text{Output level}}$$

- Unit variable costs remain the same when output varies

3.4 Fixed costs

Remember that:

- Total fixed costs remain the same, irrespective of changes in output level

- Unit fixed costs vary as output changes

    $$\text{Unit fixed cost} = \frac{\text{Total fixed cost}}{\text{Output level}}$$

Example 4

Baker Ltd is costing a single product which has the following cost details

Variable cost per unit

Materials	£5
Labour	£6
Total fixed overheads	£70,000

Complete the following total cost and unit cost table for a production level of 20,000 units. Overheads are absorbed on a per unit basis.

Element	Total cost	Unit cost
Materials	£	£
Labour	£	£
Overheads	£	£
Total	£	£

Solution

Element	Total cost	Unit cost
Materials	£100,000	£5.00
Labour	£120,000	£6.00
Overheads	£70,000	£3.50
Total	£290,000	£14.50

Workings

Materials

- This is a variable cost – unit cost is £5 (given)
- Total cost will be 20,000 units × £5 = £100,000

Labour

- This is a variable cost – unit cost is £6 (given)
- Total cost will be 20,000 units × £6 = £120,000

Overheads

- This is a fixed cost – total cost is £70,000 (given)
- Unit cost will be £70,000 ÷ 20,000 units = £3.50

Total unit cost

- This can be found by totalling the individual unit cost elements (£5 + £6 + £3.50 = £14.50), or

- Take the total cost and divide by the number of units = £290,000 ÷ 20,000 units = £14.50.

Test your understanding 8

XYZ Ltd is costing a single product which has the following cost details

Variable cost per unit

Materials	£4
Labour	£5
Total fixed costs	£60,000

Complete the following total cost and unit cost table for a production level of 15,000 units. Overheads are absorbed on a per unit basis.

Element	Total cost	Unit cost
Materials	£	£
Labour	£	£
Overheads	£	£
Total	£	£

3.5 Calculating unit costs from total costs

Sometimes in questions you might also be required to calculate the unit and total costs for a variety of different output levels, as can be seen in the following example.

Example 5

Complete the table below showing fixed costs, variable costs, total costs and unit cost at the different levels of production.

Units	Fixed costs	Variable costs	Total costs	Unit cost
1,000	£20,000	£4,000	£24,000	£24.00
2,000	£	£	£	£
3,000	£	£	£	£
4,000	£	£	£	£

Solution

Units	Fixed costs	Variable costs	Total costs	Unit cost
1,000	£20,000	£4,000	£24,000	£24.00
2,000	£20,000	£8,000	£28,000	£14.00
3,000	£20,000	£12,000	£32,000	£10.67
4,000	£20,000	£16,000	£36,000	£9.00

Workings

Fixed costs

- Unless there are stepped costs, the fixed costs will be the same at each activity level. Insert £20,000 into the fixed cost column for each activity level.

Variable costs – approach 1

- Calculate the variable cost per unit = £4,000/1,000 units = £4 per unit.

- This can then be used to get the total variable cost at different levels.

- So for 3,000 units the total variable cost will be 3,000 × £4 = £12,000.

Variable costs – approach 2

- Alternatively you could scale up the total variable cost.

- For example, going from 1,000 to 3,000 units we have increased the number of units by a factor of 3 so need to do the same to the variable costs.

- This gives total variable cost = 3 × £4,000 = £12,000 as before.

Total costs

- The total costs column is the sum of the fixed and variable costs.

Unit costs

- Simply divide the total cost by the number of units.

- E.g. for 4,000 units, unit costs = £36,000/4,000 = £9 per unit.

 Test your understanding 9

Complete the table below showing fixed costs, variable costs, total costs and unit cost at the different levels of production.

Units	Fixed costs	Variable costs	Total costs	Unit cost
1,000	£60,000	£2,000	£62,000	£62.00
2,000	£	£	£	£
3,000	£	£	£	£
4,000	£	£	£	£

 Test your understanding 10

PQR Ltd is costing a single product which has the following cost details

Variable cost per unit

Materials	£6
Labour	£8
Total fixed costs	£90,000

Complete the following total cost and unit cost table for a production level of 15,000 units. Each unit takes 2 labour hours to make, and overheads are to be absorbed into units using a rate per labour hour.

Element	Total cost	Unit cost
Materials	£	£
Labour	£	£
Overheads	£	£
Total	£	£

Test your understanding 11

ABC Ltd is costing a product which has the following cost details:

Variable cost per unit

Materials	£3
Labour	£10
Total overheads	£120,000

Complete the following total cost and unit cost table for a production level of 12,000 units. Each unit takes 0.5 machine hours to make, and overheads are to be absorbed into units using a rate per machine hour.

Element	Total cost	Unit cost
Materials	£	£
Labour	£	£
Overheads	£	£
Total	£	£

4 Other costing systems

4.1 Introduction

We've seen that the purpose of costing is to calculate the cost of each cost unit of an organisation's products. In order to do this the costs of each unit are gathered together and recorded in the costing system. This is the overall aim, but the methods and system used will differ from organisation to organisation as the type of products and production methods differ between organisations.

An organisation's cost unit might be:

- **an individual job**. Where production is made up of individual jobs, each job is given a separate identifying number and has its own job card (as seen in section 1). Effectively the job is the cost unit.

  A typical example of a business which uses job costing would be a home builder, who designs specific houses for each customer and accumulates the costs separately for each house (job). Job costing might also be used by service organisations, for example a law firm, using job costing to measure the costs of serving each individual client.

- **a batch**. Where a business produces batches of identical cost units. The total cost of the batch of production is calculated (including direct costs plus overheads) and divided by the number of units in that batch to arrive at the cost per unit for that batch.

  A typical example of a business that uses batch costing would be a baker, producing loaves of bread in batches.

- **a service**. Where an organisation provides a service rather than a product. To calculate the cost per unit the total cost of providing the service is divided by the number of service units used to provide the service.

  A typical example of a cost unit for a university might be the cost per student.

4.2 Costing in service organisations

One of the main difficulties in service costing is the establishment of a suitable cost unit. Service organisations may use several different cost units to measure the different kinds of service that they are providing.

Examples for a hotel might include:

- Meals served for the restaurant
- Rooms occupied for the cleaning staff
- Hours worked for the reception staff.

The total cost of providing a service will include the same costs as manufacturing but overheads may make up a larger proportion of the cost than direct costs. It is also possible that labour costs would be the only direct cost incurred by a service provider.

$$\text{Cost per service unit} = \frac{\text{Total costs for providing the service}}{\text{Number of service units used to provide the service}}$$

Example 6

A hotel has 100 rooms, 70% of which were occupied last week and require cleaning and maintenance. The hotel incurs the following weekly costs:

Cleaning products	£300
Repairs and maintenance	£200
Wages for cleaning staff	£3,000

The hotels' cost unit is rooms occupied.

Requirement

Calculate the average cost per room occupied.

Solution

Total costs for providing the service = £300 + £200 + £3,000 = £3,500.

Number of service units (rooms occupied) = 100 rooms × 70% = 70 rooms.

Cost per service unit = £3,500 / 70 = £50.

Test your understanding 12

Which type of organisation below is unlikely to use service costing?

A Taxi firm

B Private school

C Boat builder

D Hairdressing salon

Test your understanding 13

The accounting records for a University show the following income and expenditure for the previous term:

	£000	£000
Fee income		51,750
Salaries and wages	14,375	
Rent & rates	4,470	
Insurance	310	
Office supplies	160	
Depreciation	365	
Other overheads	445	

There were 5,750 students enrolled at the University in the term. The University's cost unit is one student.

Calculate the average cost per student and the average income per student.

Whatever the type of organisation (manufacturing or service) and whatever costing system is being used, organisations will need to forecast the expected costs of producing the job/batch or providing the service **before** the work is carried out. This forecast helps managers in setting the selling price of the job/batch/service and also provides a benchmark against which they can measure actual performance. This idea is going to be developed further in the next chapter.

5 Summary

This chapter has considered how the overheads of a business are allocated to the cost units to which they relate, using an **absorption rate**.

This will be either using a per unit basis, direct labour hour basis or a machine hour basis. This will depend on the nature of the business.

The overhead absorption rate is based upon the budgeted overheads and the budgeted production level. This rate is then used to include the overheads in the production cost throughout the accounting period.

The chapter then looked at the calculations of total and unit costs at different levels of output before moving on to consider how costing might differ in service organisations.

Possible assessment questions could require you to calculate the overhead cost per unit using the different methods, calculate the total and unit cost for a product or identify cost behaviour.

6 Further Test your understanding exercises

Test your understanding 14

Identify whether the following statements about cost behaviour are true or false.

	True	False
Variable cost per unit increases as the units of production increases.	☐	☐
Total unit cost increases as units of production increases.	☐	☐
Fixed cost per unit decreases as the units of production increases.	☐	☐

Test your understanding 15

Chiluba Ltd is costing a single product with the following cost details:

Variable costs per unit

Materials   £10

Labour   £5

Total fixed costs   £150,000

Complete the following total cost and unit cost table for a production level of 20,000 units.

Element	Total cost	Unit cost
Materials	£	£
Labour	£	£
Overheads	£	£
Total	£	£

Test your understanding 16

Complete the table below showing fixed costs, variable costs, total costs and unit cost at the different levels of production.

Units	Fixed costs	Variable costs	Total costs	Unit cost
1,000	£200,000	£5,000	£205,000	£205.00
2,000	£	£	£	£
3,000	£	£	£	£
4,000	£	£	£	£

 Test your understanding 17

Which ONE of the following is unlikely to be a valid cost unit in service costing?

A   Cost per hospital bed per night

B   Cost per motor vehicle

C   Cost per passenger mile

D   Cost per canteen meal served

Test your understanding answers

 Test your understanding 1

$$\text{Overhead} = \frac{\text{Budgeted overheads}}{\text{Budgeted units produced}} = \frac{£35,000}{1,750 \text{ units}} = £20 \text{ per unit}$$

 Test your understanding 2

Total cost per unit

Materials (5 kg × £6/kg)	£30.00
Labour (2 hours × £12/hr)	£24.00
Overheads (working)	£6.40
	£60.40

Working

$$\text{Overhead} = \frac{\text{Budgeted overheads}}{\text{Budgeted units produced}} = \frac{£80,000}{12,500 \text{ units}} = £6.40 \text{ per unit}$$

 Test your understanding 3

Overhead per unit = 1.5 hours × OAR = 1.5 × £5.60 (W1) = £8.40

(W1)

$$\text{OAR} = \frac{\text{Budgeted overheads}}{\text{Budgeted labour hours}} = \frac{£147,000}{26,250 \text{ hours (W2)}} = £5.60 \text{ per hour}$$

(W2)
Total budgeted labour hours = labour hours per unit × number of units
= 1.5 hours per unit × 17,500 units
= 26,250 hours

Test your understanding 4

Total cost per unit

Materials (7 kg × £5/kg)	£35.00
Labour (0.5 hour × £30/hr)	£15.00
Overheads (0.5 hour × £20/hr (working))	£10.00
	£60.00

Working

$$\text{Overhead} = \frac{\text{Budgeted overheads}}{\text{Budgeted labour hours}} = \frac{£120,000}{6,000 \text{ hours}} = £20 \text{ per hour}$$

 Test your understanding 5

Overhead per unit = 5 machine hours × OAR = 5 × £3.50 (W1) = £17.50

(W1)

$$\text{OAR} = \frac{\text{Budgeted overheads}}{\text{Budgeted machine hours}} = \frac{£350,000}{100,000 \text{ hours (W2)}} = £3.50 \text{ per hour}$$

(W2)
Budgeted machine hours = machine hours per unit × number of units
= 5 hours per unit × 20,000 units
= 100,000 hours

Test your understanding 6

Total cost per unit

Materials (12 kg × £4/kg)	£48.00
Labour (3 hours × £20/hr)	£60.00
Overheads (3 hours × £6/hr (working))	£18.00
	£126.00

Working

$$\text{Overhead} = \frac{\text{Budgeted overheads}}{\text{Budgeted machine hours}} = \frac{£90,000}{15,000 \text{ hours}} = £6 \text{ per hour}$$

Test your understanding 7

(a)

	Machine hour	Labour hour	Unit
Overheads (£)	200,000	200,000	200,000
Activity	10,000	80,000	8,000
Absorption rate (£)	20.00	2.50	25.00

(b)

	Machine hour £	Labour hour £	Unit £
Direct cost	25.00	25.00	25.00
Overheads	5.00	1.25	25.00
Total unit cost	30.00	26.25	50.00

Workings:

- Machine hour rate – £20 per machine hour. Each unit of Peppermint requires 15 minutes of machine time, which is 15/60 hours. The overhead absorbed is therefore £20 × 15/60 = £5.00.

- Labour hour rate – £2.50 per labour hour. Each unit of Peppermint requires 30 minutes of labour time, which is 30/60 hours. The overhead absorbed is therefore £2.50 × 30/60 = £1.25.

- Unit rate – £25 per unit. Each unit absorbs the same amount of overhead.

(c)

Based on the information provided, as we are told that Mint Ltd is a multi-product organisation, this means that the unit basis is not appropriate. This is most appropriate in organisations producing a single product.

Looking at the information for part (a), we can see that Mint Ltd has substantially more labour hours than machine hours, indicating this is a labour intensive environment. The labour hour basis would therefore be the most suitable for Mint Ltd.

Test your understanding 8

Element	Total cost	Unit cost
Materials	£60,000	£4.00
Labour	£75,000	£5.00
Overheads	£60,000	£4.00
Total	£195,000	£13.00

Test your understanding 9

Units	Fixed costs	Variable costs	Total costs	Unit cost
1,000	£60,000	£2,000	£62,000	£62.00
2,000	£60,000	£4,000	£64,000	£32.00
3,000	£60,000	£6,000	£66,000	£22.00
4,000	£60,000	£8,000	£68,000	£17.00

Test your understanding 10

Element	Total cost	Unit cost
Materials	£90,000	£6.00
Labour	£120,000	£8.00
Overheads	£90,000	£6.00
Total	£300,000	£20.00

Workings

Materials

- This is a variable cost – unit cost is £6 (given)
- Total cost will be 15,000 × £6 = £90,000

Labour

- This is a variable cost – unit cost is £8 (given)
- Total cost will be 15,000 × £ = £120,000

Overheads

- Total cost is £90,000 (given)
- Total labour hours = 15,000 units × 2 hours = 30,000 hours
- Overhead rate per labour hour = £90,000 ÷ 30,000 hours = £3.00
- Overhead cost per unit is therefore 2 hours × £3.00/hour = £6.00

Test your understanding 11

Element	Total cost	Unit cost
Materials	£36,000	£3.00
Labour	£120,000	£10.00
Overheads	£120,000	£10.00
Total	£276,000	£23.00

Workings

Materials

- This is a variable cost – unit cost is £3 (given)
- Total cost will be 12,000 × £3 = £36,000

Labour

- This is a variable cost – unit cost is £10 (given)
- Total cost will be 12,000 × £10 = £120,000

Overheads

- Total cost is £120,000 (given)
- Total machine hours = 12,000 units × 0.5 hours = 6,000 hours
- Overhead rate per machine hour = £120,000 ÷ 6,000 hours = £20
- Overhead cost per unit is therefore 0.5 hours × £20/hour = £10

 Test your understanding 12

Correct answer is C.

A boat builder is more likely to use job costing. The costs related to the manufacture of each individual boat will be easy to identify. Each boat will be a cost unit.

All other options relate to providing services and would therefore be more likely to use service costing.

 Test your understanding 13

Total University expense = £20,125,000

Total students = 5,750

Average cost per student = £20,125,000 / 5,750 = £3,500

Average income per student = £51,750,000 / 5,750 = £9,000.

Test your understanding 14

	True	False
Variable cost per unit increases as the units of production increases.	☐	☑
Total unit cost increases as units of production increases.	☐	☑
Fixed cost per unit decreases as the units of production increases.	☑	☐

Notes

- Variable cost per unit remains constant at all output levels. It is the total variable cost that would increase as production increases.

- Total unit cost decreases as units of production increase. This is because the fixed cost is spread over more units and so the fixed cost per unit falls.

- Fixed cost per unit decreases as the units of production increase as the cost is spread over more units.

Test your understanding 15

Element	Total cost	Unit cost
Materials	£200,000	£10.00
Labour	£100,000	£5.00
Overheads	£150,000	£7.50
Total	£450,000	£22.50

Test your understanding 16

Units	Fixed costs	Variable costs	Total costs	Unit cost
1,000	£200,000	£5,000	£205,000	£205.00
2,000	£200,000	£10,000	£210,000	£105.00
3,000	£200,000	£15,000	£215,000	£71.67
4,000	£200,000	£20,000	£220,000	£55.00

Test your understanding 17

Correct answer is B.

Cost per motor vehicle is more appropriate when job costing is being used.

All other options relate to providing services and would therefore be more likely to use service costing.

Budgeting and variances

Introduction

We have seen that the main purposes of management accounting are planning, control and decision making. In this chapter we will be looking in more detail at the planning and control aspects.

Planning involves organisations looking ahead and trying to forecast what is likely to happen or what the organisation would like to happen in the future. Most organisations plan using **budgets**.

Control involves reviewing what has actually happened in a period (actual results) against these plans (or budgets). The differences between actual results and budgets are called **variances.** These will be examined in detail in this chapter.

In this unit you will be required to prepare budgets, calculate variances and interpret the results. Questions might also require the use of spreadsheet functions to perform these calculations. This aspect will be covered in a later chapter.

ASSESSMENT CRITERIA	CONTENTS
Sources of information on income and expenditure (1.4)	1 Budgeting
Actual and budgeted costs and income (3.1)	2 Types of budget
	3 Variances
Exception reporting to identify significant variances (3.2)	4 Causes of variances

1 Budgeting

1.1 What is budgeting?

Budgets set out the costs and revenues that are expected to be incurred or earned in future periods.

For example, if you are planning to take a holiday, you will probably have a budgeted amount that you can spend. This budget will determine where you go and for how long.

Most organisations prepare budgets for the business as a whole. The following budgets may also be prepared by organisations:

- Departmental budgets.

- Functional budgets (for sales, production, expenditure and so on).

- Statements of profit or loss/income statements (in order to determine the expected future profits).

- Cash budgets (in order to determine future cash flows).

1.2 Budgetary control

As stated in Chapter 1, a lot of the aims of management accounting involve budgeting, as this assists managers with short-term planning and control.

- **Planning**

  The budgeting process forces managers to look ahead, set targets, anticipate problems and give the organisation purpose and direction. Budgets force organisations to plan for the future. The budget therefore provides a benchmark against which we can evaluate actual performance.

- **Control**

  The budget provides the plan against which actual results can be compared. Any difference or 'variance' between what we expected to happen (i.e. the budget) and what did happen (i.e. the actual result) can then be investigated to identify the cause. Once we know this we can take appropriate action.

1.3   Other reasons for budgeting

Other reasons for budgeting include the following:

- **Authorisation**

  A budget may act as a formal authorisation to a manager to spend a given amount on specified activities.

- **Forecasting**

  Forecasting refers to the prediction of events over which little or no control is exercised. Some parts of all budgets are, therefore, based on forecasts.

- **Communication and co-ordination**

  Budgets communicate plans to managers responsible for carrying them out. They also ensure co-ordination between managers of sub-units so that each is aware of the others' requirements.

- **Motivation**

  Budgets are often intended to motivate managers to perform in line with organisational plans and objectives.

- **Evaluation**

  The performance of managers and organisational units is often evaluated by reference to budgetary targets.

2   Types of budget

2.1   Fixed budgets

 Definition

A **fixed budget** is a budget produced for a **single** activity level.

A fixed budget will **remain the same** no matter what the actual volume of sales or production turns out to be. A fixed budget is produced at the beginning of the period and is used to provide information as to the aims and objectives that the organisation is working towards in that particular period.

However, a fixed budget is not particularly useful for control purposes. Consider the example below:

 Example 1

	Fixed budget	Actual
Units produced and sold	1,000	1,200
	£	£
Sales revenue	10,000	11,500
Material costs	1,300	1,040
Labour costs	2,600	2,125
Fixed overheads	1,950	2,200
Operating profit	4,150	6,135

The original budget was fixed, prepared at the beginning of the period, on the presumption that 1,000 units would be produced and sold.

At the end of the period, it turns out that 1,200 units were produced and sold. The results are therefore the costs and revenues of producing and selling 1,200 units. This is 200 units more than budget.

Therefore, comparing the budget for 1,000 units with the actual results for 1,200 units would not be a fair or meaningful comparison, or provide managers with useful information.

When managers are comparing the actual results with the budget for a period, it is important to ensure that they are making a valid comparison (like-for-like). The use of **flexible budgets** can help managers make more valid comparisons.

2.2 Flexible budgets

Definition

A **flexible** (or flexed) **budget** is one which, by recognising cost behaviour patterns, is designed to change as volume of activity changes.

A flexible budget should represent what the costs and revenues were expected to be at different activity levels. Comparing a flexible budget with the actual results provides management with more meaningful information for management.

Flexible budgets are produced using cost behaviour and nature principles:

- **Variable costs** increase in direct proportion to activity, i.e. as activity increases so do the costs, e.g. direct materials, direct labour.

- **Fixed costs** are constant as activity increases, e.g. overheads.

- **Sales revenue** is assumed to have a variable behaviour unless stated otherwise i.e. the more units that are sold the more revenue there is and there is a constant selling price per unit.

If we look back at the information in example 1, we can prepare a flexible budget for output of 1,200 units.

Example 2

	Fixed budget	Flexible budget (see workings)	Actual
Units produced and sold	1,000	**1,200**	1,200
	£	**£**	£
Sales revenue	10,000	**12,000**	11,500
Material costs	1,300	**1,560**	1,040
Labour costs	2,600	**3,120**	2,125
Fixed overheads	1,950	**1,950**	2,200
Operating profit	4,150	**5,370**	6,135

Workings

Sales revenue

- This is variable. If total revenue was budgeted to be £10,000 for output of 1,000 units, then the budgeted revenue per unit must be £10,000 ÷ 1,000 = £10 per unit.

- Budgeted revenue for actual output of 1,200 units will therefore be 1,200 units × £10 = £12,000.

Material costs

- This is variable. If total material costs were budgeted to be £1,300 for output of 1,000 units, then the budgeted material cost per unit must be £1,300 ÷ 1,000 = £1.30 per unit.

- Budgeted material costs for actual output of 1,200 units will therefore be 1,200 units × £1.30 = £1,560.

Labour costs

- This is variable. If total labour costs were budgeted to be £2,600 for output of 1,000 units, then the budgeted labour cost per unit must be £2,600 ÷ 1,000 = £2.60 per unit.

- Budgeted labour costs for actual output of 1,200 units will therefore be 1,200 units × £2.60 = £3,120.

Fixed overheads

- This is fixed and will not change with changes in the level of activity. We therefore include the same value in the budget for 1,200 units.

Test your understanding 1

Squash Ltd makes orange juice. Each bottle of orange juice requires the juice from 25 oranges, at a cost of £0.10 per orange.

(a) Calculate direct material cost per bottle.

(b) Calculate the budgeted material cost of producing 12 bottles of juice.

Test your understanding 2

Vita Ltd is preparing its budget for the next quarter and it needs to consider different production levels.

Complete the table below to calculate the flexible budgets for 1,500 units and 2,000 units.

Units sold and produced	1,000	1,500	2,000
Sales revenue	40,000		
Variable costs:			
Direct materials	4,000		
Direct labour	3,800		
Fixed overhead	10,700		
Total cost	18,500		
Total profit	21,500		

2.3 Budget calculations

In your exam you may be required to prepare a budget for a single product organisation, using unit cost information. You may also need to use an interactive table, simulating a spreadsheet, in order to do this. We will cover this in the later chapter on spreadsheets.

 Example 3

Fountain Ltd is a manufacturer of garden ornaments. You have been provided with the following budgeted information.

Complete the budget below for production of 2,000 units to calculate the budgeted profit or loss for the period.

Budget information	
Selling price	£20 per unit
Budgeted production	2,000 units
Production overheads	£12,000
Materials	500 kgs @ £15 per kg
Labour	1,500 hours @ £12 per hour

	Budget £ 2,000 units
Revenue	
Direct materials	
Direct labour	
Production overheads	
Profit/loss	

Solution:

	Budget £ 2,000 units
Revenue	40,000
Direct materials	7,500
Direct labour	18,000
Production overheads	12,000
Profit / loss	2,500

Workings

Revenue: 2,000 units × £20 = £40,000

Direct materials: 500 kgs × £15 per kg = £7,500

Direct labour: 1,500 hours × £12 per hour = £18,000

Production overheads: Fixed at £12,000

 Test your understanding 3

Roly Ltd is a watch manufacturer. You have been provided with the following budgeted information.

Complete the budget to calculate the budgeted profit or loss for the period.

Budget information	
Selling price	£80 per unit
Budgeted production	3,500 units
Production overheads	£36,000
Materials	200 kgs @ £35 per kg
Labour	3,800 hours @ £25 per hour

	Budget £ 3,500 units
Revenue	
Direct materials	
Direct labour	
Production overheads	
Profit/loss	

3 Variances

3.1 What is a variance?

The difference between actual and expected (or budgeted) costs or income is known as a variance.

 Definition

An **adverse variance** occurs when the actual costs exceed the budgeted costs or when the actual revenue is less than the budgeted revenue.

A **favourable variance** occurs when the actual cost is less than the budgeted cost or when the actual revenue exceeds the budgeted revenue.

3.2 How to calculate a variance

For Principles of Costing the only calculations required will be a comparison of actual costs or revenues with the expected costs or revenues in a **fixed budget**.

Example 4

Fujimori Ltd has produced a performance report detailing budgeted and actual material cost for last month.

Calculate the amount of the variance and then determine whether it is adverse or favourable by putting a tick in the relevant column of the table below.

Cost type	Budget £	Actual £	Variance £	Adv.	Fav.
Materials	24,500	26,200		☐	☐

Solution

Cost type	Budget £	Actual £	Variance £	Adv.	Fav.
Materials	24,500	26,200	1,700	☑	☐

Notes

- Variance = actual – budget = £26,200 – £24,500 = £1,700
- The variance is adverse as **the actual cost is higher** than budgeted.

 Example 5

Sushi Ltd has produced a performance report detailing budgeted and actual sales revenue for last year.

Calculate the amount of the variance and then determine whether it is adverse or favourable by putting a tick in the relevant column of the table below.

Cost type	Budget £	Actual £	Variance £	Adv.	Fav.
Sales	17,500	16,950		☐	☐

Solution

Cost type	Budget £	Actual £	Variance £	Adv.	Fav.
Sales	17,500	16,950	550	☑	☐

Notes

- Variance = £16,950 – £17,00 = £550
- The variance is adverse as the **actual revenue is lower** than budgeted.

Test your understanding 4

Identify the following statements as being true or false by putting a tick in the relevant column of the table below.

Statement	True	False
A variance is the difference between budgeted and actual cost.	☐	☐
A favourable variance means budgeted costs are greater than actual costs.	☐	☐
An adverse variance means you have made a saving compared to budgeted costs.	☐	☐

Test your understanding 5

Kagame Ltd has produced a performance report detailing budgeted and actual cost for last month.

Calculate the amount of the variance for each cost type and then determine whether it is adverse or favourable by putting a tick in the relevant column of the table below.

	Budget £	Actual £	Variance £	Adv.	Fav.
Revenue	125,000	137,000		☐	☐
Materials	56,000	49,500		☐	☐
Labour	64,000	65,200		☐	☐
Overheads	150,000	148,500		☐	☐

3.3 Evaluating the significance of a variance

Management do not want to waste time investigating small or insignificant variances, and so will set criteria for deciding what makes a variance large enough to report and investigate.

For example:

- 'Only investigate variances bigger than £500' or

- 'Only investigate variances bigger than 5% of budget'

If using a percentage measure then the amount of the variance that exceeds the cut-off percentage is known as the 'discrepancy'.

$$\text{Variance as a \% of budget} = \frac{\text{variance}}{\text{budget}} \times 100$$

 Test your understanding 6

The purchasing manager at Globe Ltd has discovered that actual direct material costs for the previous month were £36,450. The budget for direct materials was £38,200.

Calculate the percentage variance to two decimal places.

 Test your understanding 7

The sales manager at Globe Ltd has produced a performance report detailing budgeted and actual sales revenue for this month. Any variance in excess of 5% of budget is deemed to be significant.

The Southern division has reported actual revenues of £576,000. The budget for the Southern division was £595,000.

Determine whether the variance for the Southern division is significant or not.

Example 6

Antrobus Ltd has produced a performance report detailing budgeted and actual material cost for last month. Any variance in excess of 10% of budget is deemed to be significant and should be reviewed.

Calculate the amount of the variance and then determine whether it is significant by putting a tick in the relevant column of the table below.

Cost type	Budget £	Actual £	Variance £	Significant	Not significant
Labour	5,600	5,200		☐	☐

Solution

Cost type	Budget £	Actual £	Variance £	Significant	Not significant
Labour	5,600	5,200	400	☐	☑

Workings

- Variance = £5,200 – £5,600 = £400

- As a % of budget this gives (400/5,600) × 100 = 7.1%, which is less than 10%, so the variance is deemed not significant.

 Test your understanding 8

G Ltd has produced a performance report detailing budgeted and actual cost for this month. Any variance in excess of 5% of budget is deemed to be significant and should be reported to the relevant manager.

Examine the variances in the table below and indicate whether they are significant or not by putting a tick in the relevant column.

Cost type	Budget £	Variance £	Significant	Not significant
Direct materials	26,000	1,200	☐	☐
Direct labour	35,000	2,000	☐	☐
Production overheads	15,000	1,100	☐	☐
Selling costs	2,000	90	☐	☐

Test your understanding 9

Jonas Ltd has produced a performance report detailing budgeted and actual cost for this month. Any variance in excess of 5% of budget is deemed to be significant and should be reported to the relevant manager.

Examine the variances in the table below, calculate the variance as a percentage of budget, rounded to two decimal places, and then determine whether they are significant (S) or Not Significant (NS) in the relevant column.

Cost type	Budget £	Variance £	%	S or NS
Direct materials	24,000	1,600		
Direct labour	45,000	1,800		
Production overheads	19,000	1,750		
Selling costs	1,900	70		

 Test your understanding 10

Sparkle Ltd is a manufacturer of mirrors. You have been provided with the following budgeted information, based on the production of 1,800 units.

Budget:
- Sales price: £55 per unit
- Direct materials: 720 kgs costing £20 per kg
- Direct labour: 1,100 hours costing £15 per hour
- Production overheads: £35,000

Complete the table below to calculate the budgeted profit or loss for the period and variance information. Variance percentages should be provided to two decimal places.

	Budget £ 1,800 units	Actual £ 2,000 units	Variance	Variance %
Revenue		90,000		
Direct materials		17,280		
Direct labour		18,700		
Overheads		26,000		
Profit / loss		28,020		

3.4 Reporting variances

Actions and their consequences should be traced to the person responsible. This may give the impression of 'laying the blame', but it is equally possible to award praise (and remunerate accordingly).

Responsibility accounting is a system which recognises various decision centres within a business and traces costs (and possibly revenues) to the individual managers who are primarily responsible for making decisions about the items in question.

You may be asked in your assessment on the appropriateness of reporting a particular variance to a suggested manager.

For example, reporting sales variances to the sales manager would make sense, as he/she is then in the right position to be able to act on such information. If an adverse variance has occurred this period, it makes sense to try to ensure that it does not occur again next period.

It should be noted that a decision could result in either a favourable or an adverse variance, and that the overall picture should be the basis for subsequent action.

 Example 7

A purchasing manager is looking to place an order to buy fresh direct materials. Instead of ordering from the usual supplier, she is made aware that a different supplier will charge a much lower price than the business usually pays. If this then results in a favourable direct material cost variance, the purchasing manager has acted well and should be praised accordingly.

However, if the reason for the low price is that the materials are of much lower quality, with the result that there is much greater than usual wastage, this might produce overall an adverse variance. Accordingly, the purchasing manager should not buy from that supplier again.

✍ Test your understanding 11

Identify the following statements as being true or false by putting a tick in the relevant column of the table below.

Statement	True	False
The variance for the direct material cost of Department A should be reported to the purchasing manager.	☐	☐
The variance for the direct labour cost of Department B should be reported to the production manager of Department A.	☐	☐
The variance for sales revenue should be reported to the sales manager.	☐	☐
The adverse variance for the direct labour cost of Department A should be reported to the Human Resources manager, who agreed pay rises for all production staff.	☐	☐

✍ Test your understanding 12

You have been provided with the following information related to last month's performance.

Cost type	Budget £	Actual £	Variance %	S / NS	Report to
Sales revenue	30,000	33,600			
Direct labour	12,000	15,500			
Direct materials	6,500	6,800			

Reporting policies state that:

- Variances in excess of 5% of budget, and that are greater than £500, are significant and should be reported to the department manager (DM).

- Adverse variances in excess of 10% of budget, and that are greater than £2,000, are significant and should be reported to the department director (DD).

- Variances in excess of 20% of budget, and that are greater than £3,000, are significant and should be reported to the department director (DD).

Complete the table above to show each variance percentage, identifying whether each variance is significant or now and who (if anyone) the variance should be reported to.

4 Causes of variances

4.1 Introduction

Differences between actual values and budgeted values can occur for a number of reasons.

One of the main reasons is that when producing a budget we are trying to predict the future. Prediction of the future is not an exact science and it is therefore extremely difficult to get it 100% correct.

This leads to the budgeted figures not being as accurate as they could be and therefore actual values are different from these.

4.2 Sales variances

A sales variance could occur for a number of reasons:

- **Price changes** – selling the product at a higher or lower price. This could happen if **discounts** are offered to the customer or discounts are removed or reduced, a price drop is required to remain **competitive** and/or an enforced price change due to **legislation**.

- **Volume changes** – higher or lower volumes are sold than expected. This could be due to a successful or unsuccessful **advertising** campaign; changes in buyers' **habits**; a problem with production may reduce availability and/or changes in **market conditions**.

4.3 Material variances

A material variance can have a number of causes when we consider the raw material used to produce the product:

- **Price changes** – an increase or decrease in the price per unit of **material** purchased. This could be due to suppliers changing prices, loss or introduction of a **bulk discount**, higher delivery charges and/or a change in the **quality** of the material (a higher price would be presumed to result in a higher quality material).

- **Usage changes** – an increase or decrease in the amount of material used. This could be due to more **efficient** or less efficient working conditions and/or a change in the **quality** of the materials purchased.

- **Combination of quality and quantity**. Higher quality costs more but may well lead to less wastage so use less. Lower quality costs less but may lead to more wastage so use more.

4.4 Labour variances

Variances in labour costs can be caused by:

- **Rate changes** – a higher or lower hourly rate is paid to the employees than expected. If a **higher grade** of labour is used then they will require **higher remuneration**. If a **lower grade** of labour is used then they will require **lower remuneration**. There could be an increase in the basic rate of pay (minimum wage) or a bonus may have been paid.

- **Efficiency** of staff or the **hours worked** to produce output. If the actual time taken is **longer** than budgeted then this will **cost more** but if actual time taken is **shorter** than budgeted then it will **cost less**. This could be due to change in the grade of labour as the more experience the staff the more efficient they are assumed to be.

- **Overtime**. If there is extra time needed to complete the production then this may have to lead to having to pay some staff overtime. This is often paid at a **higher rate** than normal hours. This will **increase** the labour costs due to both increased hours and increased rates of pay.

4.5 Fixed overheads variances

Fixed overheads should not change when activity levels change so the cause of any variance when comparing the flexed and actual figures is due to the budgeted **expenditure** being different from actual expenditure.

4.6 Possible courses of action for correction of variances

Following are a number of possible solutions for variances that arise:

- **Adverse sales variance** - lower the price of the finished goods to increase volume of sales or increase advertising to improve sales volumes without impacting on sales price.

- **Adverse materials variance** – change to a cheaper supplier, negotiate buying discounts, purchase better quality materials so there is less wastage.

- **Adverse labour variances** – better supervision of staff to reduce idle time or increase training to make staff more efficient.

- **General variances** - closer monitoring of budgets may make the budgets more accurate.

This list is not exhaustive and it would be necessary to take each variance in turn and investigate the best way to improve the situation.

Test your understanding 13

Identify the following statements as being true or false by putting a tick in the relevant column of the table below.

Statement	True	False
Reducing the selling price of a product will result in a sales variance.	☐	☐
Using a higher quality of materials will result in a favourable materials variance.	☐	☐
Renting cheaper head office premises will result in a favourable fixed overhead variance.	☐	☐
Planning errors will always result in adverse variances.	☐	☐

Test your understanding 14

A company has a higher than expected staff turnover and as a result staff are less experienced than expected. As an indirect result of this, are the labour rate variances and the material usage variances likely to be adverse or favourable?

	Labour rate	Materials usage
A	Favourable	Favourable
B	Adverse	Favourable
C	Favourable	Adverse
D	Adverse	Adverse

Test your understanding 15

Delia Ltd had budgeted profits of £5,370 for this month. The management accountant has prepared the actual results for the month and calculated the following variances:

	Variance £
Sales revenue	500 A
Material costs	520 F
Labour costs	995 F
Fixed overheads	250 A

Calculate the actual profit made in the month.

5 Summary

In this chapter we began by looking at budgeting and how to use knowledge of cost behaviours to predict costs at given activity levels in the production of fixed and flexible budgets.

The chapter then moved on to determine variances through the comparison of actual results with budget, noting whether the variance is adverse or favourable. It also looked at the significance of variances, and to whom they should be reported.

Another important aspect of this chapter is analysis of variances including possible causes and effects of these variances.

It will be necessary in the assessment to be able to identify cost behaviours and use them to produce a budget, which will then be used to calculate variances. A question might also require the use of spreadsheet functions in these calculations. This will be covered in a later chapter.

6 Further Test your understanding exercises

Test your understanding 16

Ben Ali Ltd has produced a performance report detailing budgeted and actual cost for last month.

Calculate the amount of the variance for each cost type and then determine whether it is adverse or favourable by putting a tick in the relevant column of the table below.

Cost type	Budget £	Actual £	Variance £	Adv.	Fav.
Sales	175,000	176,850		☐	☐
Labour	15,000	14,950		☐	☐
Overheads	120,600	120,000		☐	☐

Test your understanding 17

Identify the following statements as being true or false by putting a tick in the relevant column of the table below.

Statement	True	False
A variance is the difference between actual and budgeted cost.	☐	☐
A variance is the average of actual and budgeted cost.	☐	☐
A favourable variance means this cost element would reduce profit compared to budget.	☐	☐
An adverse variance means you have made a saving compared to budgeted costs.	☐	☐

KAPLAN PUBLISHING

Test your understanding 18

Ionatana Ltd has produced a performance report detailing budgeted and actual material cost for last month. Any variance in excess of 6% of budget is deemed to be significant and should be reviewed.

Calculate the amount of the variance and then determine whether it is significant by putting a tick in the relevant column of the table below.

Cost type	Budget	Actual	Variance	Significant?	
	£	£	£	Yes	No
Direct labour	10,000	9,500		☐	☐
Direct materials	13,000	15,200		☐	☐
Production overheads	24,000	25,120		☐	☐
Administration costs	35,000	32,400		☐	☐
Selling and distribution costs	45,000	49,260		☐	☐

Test your understanding 19

You have been provided with the following information related to last month's performance.

	Budgeted £	Actual £
Labour costs	145,000	162,400

In addition to this, you are told that:

- Variances in excess of 5% of budget, and that are greater than £5,000, are significant and should be reported to the department manager.

- Adverse variances in excess of 10% of budget, and that are greater than £20,000, are significant and should be reported to the department director.

Calculate the following:

(a) The variance on labour costs.

(b) The percentage labour cost variance to TWO decimal places.

(c) Whether the variance is adverse or favourable.

(d) Whether the variance is significant or not.

(e) Who (if anyone) the variance should be reported to.

Test your understanding answers

Test your understanding 1

Squash Ltd makes orange juice. Each bottle of orange juice requires the juice from 25 oranges, at a cost of £0.10 per orange.

(a) 25 oranges × £0.10 per orange = £2.50

(b) 12 bottles × £2.50 = £30

Test your understanding 2

Units sold and produced	1,000	1,500	2,000
Sales revenue	40,000	60,000	80,000
Variable costs:			
Direct materials	4,000	6,000	8,000
Direct labour	3,800	5,700	7,600
Fixed overhead	10,700	10,700	10,700
Total cost	18,500	22,400	26,300
Total profit/ (loss)	21,500	37,600	53,700

Workings

- Sales revenue is variable, £40,000 ÷ 1,000 = £40 per unit.

- Direct materials are variable, £4,000 ÷ 1,000 = £4 per unit.

- Direct labour is variable, £3,800 ÷ 1,000 = £3.80 per unit.

- Fixed overhead is fixed at £10,700 for all activity levels.

Test your understanding 3

	Budget £ **3,500 units**
Revenue	280,000
Direct materials	7,000
Direct labour	95,000
Production overheads	36,000
Profit / loss	142,000

Workings

Revenue

- 3,500 units × £80 = £280,000

Direct materials

- 200 kgs × £35 per kg = £7,000

Direct labour

- 3,800 hours × £25 per hour = £95,000

Production overheads

- Fixed at £36,000

Test your understanding 4

Statement	True	False
A variance is the difference between budgeted and actual cost.	☑	☐
A favourable variance means budgeted costs are greater than actual costs.	☑	☐
An adverse variance means you have made a saving compared to budgeted costs.	☐	☑

Test your understanding 5

	Budget £	Actual £	Variance £	Adv.	Fav.
Revenue	125,000	137,000	12,000	☐	☑
Materials	56,000	49,500	6,500	☐	☑
Labour	64,000	65,200	1,200	☑	☐
Overheads	150,000	148,500	1,500	☐	☑

Test your understanding 6

Percentage variance $= \dfrac{\text{Variance}}{\text{Budget}} \times 100 = \dfrac{£38,200 - £36,450}{£38,200} \times 100 = 4.58\%$

Test your understanding 7

Percentage variance $= \dfrac{£576,000 - £595,000}{£595,000} \times 100 = 3.19\%$

As this is less than 5%, this is not significant.

Test your understanding 8

Cost type	Budget £	Variance £	Significant	Not significant
Direct materials	26,000	1,200	☐	☑
Direct labour	35,000	2,000	☑	☐
Production overheads	15,000	1,100	☑	☐
Selling costs	2,000	90	☐	☑

Workings

- Materials $(1,200/26,000) \times 100 = 4.6\%$
- Labour $(2,000/35,000) \times 100 = 5.7\%$
- Overheads $(1,100/15,000) \times 100 = 7.3\%$
- Selling costs $(90/2,000) \times 100 = 4.5\%$

Test your understanding 9

Cost type	Budget £	Variance £	%	S or NS
Direct materials	24,000	1,600	6.67	S
Direct labour	45,000	1,800	4.00	NS
Production overheads	19,000	1,750	9.21	S
Selling costs	1,900	70	3.68	NS

Test your understanding 10

	Budget £ 1,800 units	Actual £ 2,000 units	Variance	Variance %
Revenue	99,000	90,000	9,000	9.09
Direct materials	14,400	17,280	2,880	20.00
Direct labour	16,500	18,700	2,200	13.33
Overheads	35,000	26,000	9,000	25.71
Profit / loss	33,100	28,020	5,080	15.35

Test your understanding 11

Statement	True	False
The variance for the direct material cost of Department A should be reported to the purchasing manager.	☑	☐
The variance for the direct labour cost of Department B should be reported to the production manager of Department A.	☐	☑
The variance for sales revenue should be reported to the sales manager.	☑	☐
The adverse variance for the direct labour cost of Department A should be reported to the Human Resources manager, who agreed pay rises for all production staff.	☑	☐

Test your understanding 12

Cost type	Budget £	Actual £	Variance %	S / NS	Report to
Sales revenue	30,000	33,600	12.00	S	DM
Direct labour	12,000	15,500	29.17	S	DD
Direct materials	6,500	6,800	4.62	NS	–

Workings

Sales revenue

- Variance percentage = (33,600 – 30,000)/30,000 = 12%.

- This is a favourable variance and so does not fit into the second category, as that is only for adverse variances. It is, however, greater than 5% and greater than £500 and so falls into the first category. It is significant and should be reported to the DM.

Direct labour

- Variance percentage = (15,500 – 12,000)/12,000 = 29.17%.

- This is greater than 20% and greater than £3,000 and so falls into the third category. It is significant and should be reported to the DD.

Direct materials

- Variance percentage = (6,800 – 6,500)/6,500 = 4.62%.

- This is less than 5% and so is not significant and does not need to be reported to anyone.

Test your understanding 13

Statement	True	False
Reducing the selling price of a product will result in a sales variance.	☑	☐
Using a higher quality of materials will result in a favourable materials variance.	☐	☑
Renting cheaper head office premises will result in a favourable fixed overhead variance.	☑	☐
Planning errors will always result in adverse variances.	☐	☑

- Reducing the selling price will result in a sales variance. Less revenue will be generated per unit sold, which may also result in increased units being sold.

- Using a higher quality of material may be more expensive. This is likely to result in an adverse materials variance, as materials will cost more than planned.

- Renting cheaper premises than planned will result in the fixed overheads being less than budget. This is a favourable variance.

- Planning errors will lead to errors in the budget. These may result in either adverse or favourable variances, depending on why the original budget was incorrect.

Test your understanding 14

C

Less experienced staff are likely to be paid at a lower rate and therefore the labour rate variance will be favourable.

Usage of materials is likely to be adverse as the staff are less experienced, therefore there will be more wastage and a higher level of rejects.

 Test your understanding 15

Remember that:

- Adverse variances decrease the budgeted profit, so this is subtracted from the budgeted profit.

- Favourable variances increase the budgeted profit, so this is added to the budgeted profit.

		Variance	
Budgeted profit			**£5,370**
Sales revenue	Adverse, so deduct	500 A	
Material costs	Favourable, so add	520 F	
Labour costs	Favourable, so add	995 F	
Fixed overheads	Adverse, so deduct	250 A	
Actual profit			**£6,135**

Test your understanding 16

Cost type	Budget £	Actual £	Variance £	Adv.	Fav.
Sales	175,000	176,850	1,850	☐	☑
Labour	15,000	14,950	50	☐	☑
Overheads	120,600	120,000	600	☐	☑

Test your understanding 17

Statement	True	False
A variance is the difference between actual and budgeted cost.	☑	☐
A variance is the average of actual and budgeted cost.	☐	☑
A favourable variance means this cost element would reduce profit compared to budget.	☐	☑
An adverse variance means you have made a saving compared to budgeted costs.	☐	☑

Test your understanding 18

Cost type	Budget £	Actual £	Variance £	Significant? Yes	No
Direct labour	10,000	9,500	500	☐	☑
Direct materials	13,000	15,200	2,200	☑	☐
Production overheads	24,000	25,120	1,120	☐	☑
Administration costs	35,000	32,400	2,600	☑	☐
Selling and distribution costs	45,000	49,260	4,260	☑	☐

Test your understanding 19

(a)   Variance on labour costs = £162,400 – £145,000 = £17,400

(b)   Percentage labour cost variance = variance/budget × 100
       = £17,400/£145,000 × 100 = 12.00%

(c)   Actual labour costs were greater than budget, therefore the variance is adverse.

(d)   The variance percentage is greater than 5% of budget, and therefore will be considered significant.

(e)   The variance percentage is in excess of 10% of budget and is adverse. However, it is not in excess of £20,000 and so the second bullet does not apply. The variance therefore needs to be reported to the department manager.

Introduction to spreadsheets

Introduction

There are many different spreadsheet applications available which can be used to support the cost calculations we have seen in previous chapters. Microsoft Excel is by far the most commonly used, and this chapter is written using Microsoft Excel 2016. In your assessment, however, it will not be Excel which you will be using; you will be provided with an interactive screen, which has some of the basic functionality of Excel.

This chapter will guide you through the structure of the worksheet and how to enter and format data. You will also learn how to use basic formulas, such as addition and multiplication, to support cost calculations.

In your assessment, you should expect to see two tasks which will draw upon these spreadsheet skills. In one of the tasks you will need to enter and format data, and in the second task you will be required to create and use formulas.

ASSESSMENT CRITERIA	CONTENTS
Enter and format data (4.1) Use formulas to support cost calculations (4.2)	1 Introduction to spreadsheets 2 Entering data 3 Formatting cells 4 Formatting numbers 5 Using formulas

1 Introduction to spreadsheets

1.1 The worksheet

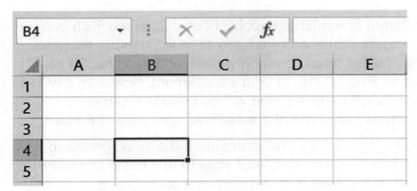

The spreadsheet (worksheet) shown above is made up of 'rows', 'columns' and 'cells':

- The 'rows' are numbered down the left hand-side from 1 onwards.

- The 'columns' are lettered along the top from A onwards.

- The 'cells' are the junction of columns and rows [example cell A1 is the junction of column A and row 1].

- The 'active' cell is where you are be able to enter data and is highlighted with a bold border [See cell B4 above]. Both the column letter (B) and the row number (4) are also highlighted.

1.2 Selecting single cells

To select a cell, left-click on the cell you wish to select. This is now the **active cell**. The value or formula in the active cell will be shown in the **formula bar**, and the **cell reference** will be shown in the **name box**.

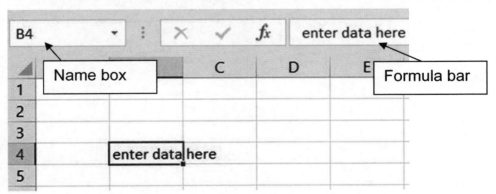

1.3 Selecting multiple cells

Selecting several cells at once is easiest using the mouse.

- Using the mouse, **left-click** on a cell to select it, but **HOLD DOWN** the mouse button

- **DRAG** the mouse pointer to select neighbouring cells.

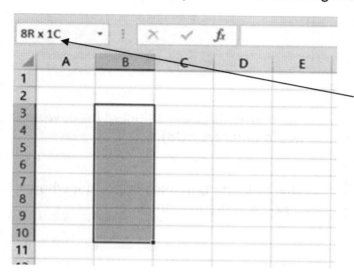

While the mouse button is held down, the dimensions of the box chosen will be shown in the name box – this will disappear when the mouse button is released.

If you wish to select non-contiguous (not neighbouring) cells, press the **Ctrl** key while selecting individual cells.

To select **ALL** cells in a worksheet, click on the box in the top-left of the sheet, to the left of Column A and above Row 1.

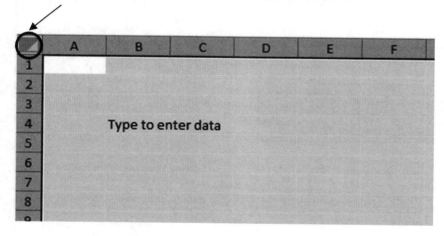

1.4 Cell ranges

As we have seen, each cell in Excel has a name, for example A1 or B7. If you select multiple cells, this is known as a **RANGE** of cells. If you select two separate cells, for example C2 and E5, the cells would be separated by a comma, so this would be displayed as **(C2, E5)**. If, as is more common, a **BLOCK** of cells is selected, these are displayed as:

(Top left cell: Bottom right cell)

For example:

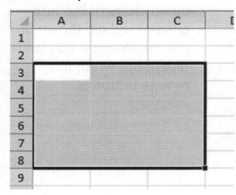

To refer to the cells selected here, we would enter **(A3:C8)**.

This notation becomes important when we deal with functions later.

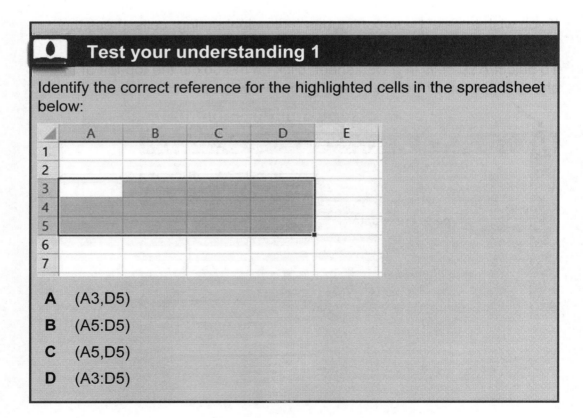

Test your understanding 1

Identify the correct reference for the highlighted cells in the spreadsheet below:

A   (A3,D5)

B   (A5:D5)

C   (A5,D5)

D   (A3:D5)

2 Entering data

2.1 Entering data

To enter data into the active cell, simply type the data required into the cell – either numeric or text. This will overwrite any existing data.

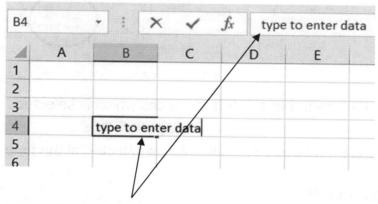

As you type, the data will be displayed on the spreadsheet itself and within the formula bar.

2.2 Editing existing data

If a cell already contains data and you wish to edit it without overwriting, there are two ways to do this, via the formula bar or directly in the cell:

1 **Double click** on a cell to edit it, or

2 With the cell selected, **left-click** in the **formula bar** to edit its contents.

2.3 Deleting data

To **delete** cell content you can do the following

1 Go to the cell you wish to delete. Press the delete key. You can highlight multiple cells and delete in the same way.

2 'Right-click' in the active cell and then 'left-click' **clear contents.** You can highlight multiple adjacent cells and delete in the same way.

2.4 Inserting and deleting rows and columns

You can insert rows and columns into your worksheet. You can also delete rows and columns from your worksheet.

To add or remove a row or column to your worksheet:

- Select '**Insert**' or '**Delete**'

- Select either '**Insert Sheet Rows/Columns**' or '**Delete Sheet Rows/Columns**'

- New columns will be inserted **to the left** of the cell which is selected at the time

- New rows will be inserted **above** the cell which is selected at the time

2.5 Copy and paste cells

Excel allows you to copy data from the 'active cell(s)' to other cells.

- Click on the cell you wish to copy

- Press the '**Copy**' button.   This will create a copy of the cell(s) you want to copy.

- You now need to tell the spreadsheet where you want to place this copy. This requires you to '**paste**' the data to a new location. Click to select the cell (or cells) where you wish to copy the contents to

- Press the '**Paste**' button

3 Formatting cells

3.1 Introduction

Formatting is a process whereby you change the visual aspects of the contents in your worksheet.

The types of formatting you are required to be able to perform are:

1 Formatting cells, e.g. bold, italics, underline, merge, fill with colour, wrap text, text size and borders.

2 Formatting numbers, e.g. thousand separators, accountancy, percentages and decimals.

The **Format Cells** menu in Excel has many in-depth formatting capabilities. You may wish to investigate this further as a part of your own studies in Excel.

However, for the purpose of your assessment, the formatting tools that you will be required to use will be found in the ribbon along the top of the interactive screen. Whilst in your assessment the icons may appear in a different order, or with a slightly different image, to the ones we will look at in Excel, they will be easy to identify and use having reviewed the notes in this chapter.

3.2 Font

If you are required to change the format of the font in a particular cell or cells, then you would firstly click on the cell(s) and then select on the appropriate formatting option:

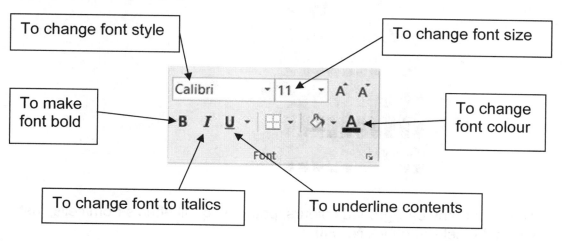

3.3 Borders

As the name suggests, this allows you to place a border around a cell or cells, to improve the look of the spreadsheet, or highlight important cells.

Firstly, highlight the cell(s) which you wish to place a border around. Click on the 'borders' icon and the appropriate border can then be selected directly from here:

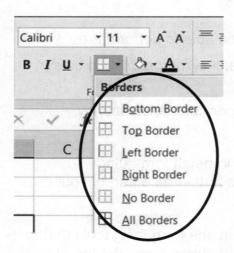

3.4 Fill with colour

The 'fill' tool can be used to highlight data in cells or to change the background colour or pattern of cells.

Select the cell or selection of cells you wish to highlight, select a colour from the options and click OK.

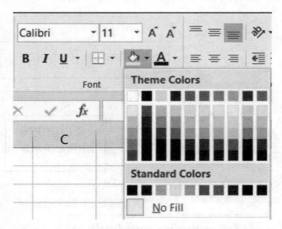

To remove any background colours, patterns, or fill effects from cells, just select the cells and pick **No Fill**.

3.5 Alignment

The **Alignment** tab allows you to choose whereabouts in a cell the text will be displayed, as well as giving the options to wrap text or merge cells.

3.6 Wrap text

This feature allows all of the contents of a cell to be displayed in the one cell, without it overflowing into other cells. It does this by creating multiple lines within the cell, rather than it all being presented on one long line.

Consider the following example. In the heading in cell A1, we can see that the words 'Pearl Ltd Budget for 20X9' overflow into cells B1 and C1.

	A	B	C	D
1	Pearl Ltd Budget for 20X9			
2				
3		**Budget**	**Actual**	**Variance**
4	Sales	120,000	130,000	10,000
5	Materials	30,000	35,000	-5,000
6	Labour	40,000	36,000	4,000
7	Overheads	10,000	11,000	-1,000
8	Profit	40,000	48,000	8,000

If we wish to 'wrap' the text, we select the cell that we wish to wrap (A1 here) and then click on the 'wrap text' icon: ⧉ Wrap Text

The contents of the cell will now appear over two or more rows within the single cell:

	A	B	C	D
1	Pearl Ltd Budget for 20X9			
2				
3		**Budget**	**Actual**	**Variance**
4	Sales	120,000	130,000	10,000
5	Materials	30,000	35,000	-5,000
6	Labour	40,000	36,000	4,000
7	Overheads	10,000	11,000	-1,000
8	Profit	40,000	48,000	8,000

3.7 Merge cells

Merging cells combines two or more cells to create one new, larger cell. This can be useful for headings that relate to more than one column.

Consider the previous example we had for the budget of Pearl Ltd. We may decide that the heading would be more prominent, and look more professional, if it was centred across all of the columns to which it relates (so columns A-D). This can be done as follows:

- Firstly, select the cells you wish to merge (A1:D1)

	A	B	C	D
1	Pearl Ltd Budget for 20X9			
2				
3		Budget	Actual	Variance
4	Sales	120,000	130,000	10,000
5	Materials	30,000	35,000	-5,000
6	Labour	40,000	36,000	4,000
7	Overheads	10,000	11,000	-1,000
8	Profit	40,000	48,000	8,000

- Then click the 'merge and center' icon: 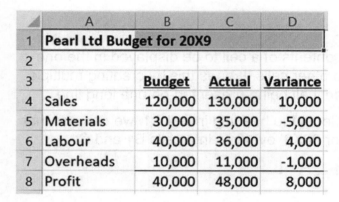 Merge & Center ▾

The cells will now be treated as one big cell from A to D and the text will appear in the centre of these merged cells:

	A	B	C	D
1	Pearl Ltd Budget for 20X9			
2				
3		Budget	Actual	Variance
4	Sales	120,000	130,000	10,000
5	Materials	30,000	35,000	-5,000
6	Labour	40,000	36,000	4,000
7	Overheads	10,000	11,000	-1,000
8	Profit	40,000	48,000	8,000

Note that if your screen has only the 'merge' icon as a separate tool, you would firstly need to merge the cells, and would then 'centre' the contents using the alignment image showing below:

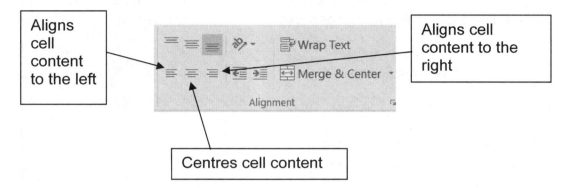

Aligns cell content to the left

Aligns cell content to the right

Centres cell content

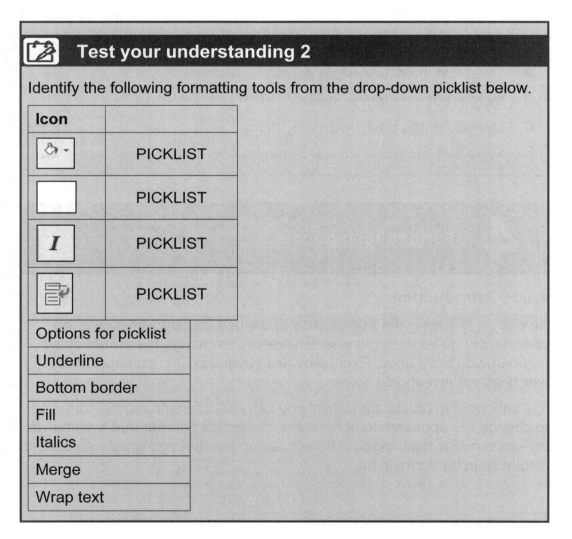

Test your understanding 2

Identify the following formatting tools from the drop-down picklist below.

Icon	
	PICKLIST
	PICKLIST
I	PICKLIST
	PICKLIST

Options for picklist
Underline
Bottom border
Fill
Italics
Merge
Wrap text

Test your understanding 3

Identify which one of the following options correctly shows all of the formatting tools which have been used in cells A1:D1 below:

	A	B	C	D
1	*Stellios Ltd Budget 20X4*			
2				
3		Budget	Actual	Variance
4	Sales	1200	1400	200
5	Materials	300	370	-70
6	Labour	230	280	-50
7	Overheads	180	210	-30
8	Profit	490	540	50

A   Wrap text, bold, underline, italics

B   Merge, bold, underline, italics

C   Merge, centre, bold, underline, italics

D   Wrap text, centre, bold, underline, italics

4 Formatting numbers

4.1 Introduction

As well as changing the appearance of the text content within cells, an assessment question might also require you to change the format of the numbers you have used. Excel provides several built-in number formats which we will investigate below.

It is important to realise that whilst you can use different number formats to change the appearance of numbers, the actual number that is written in the cell remains unchanged. The actual number that you initially entered is displayed in the formula bar.

To illustrate the different number formats that you need to be aware of, we will work through them using the value 5102 in cell B3, as showing below:

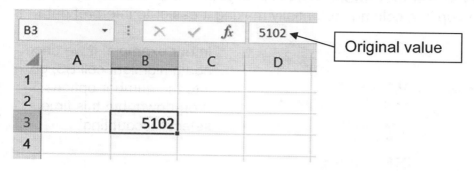

Original value

4.2 Number

To change the value to 'number' format, first of all select cell B3. In Excel, then click in the drop-down menu in the 'Number' tab.

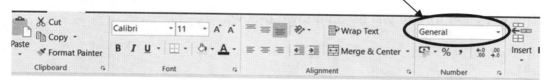

Select 'Number':

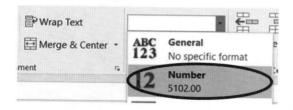

This will change the contents of the cell to the format showing below:

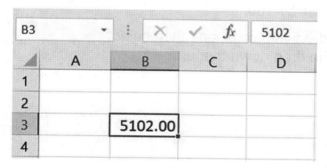

4.3   Accounting

This is very similar to **Number**, but decimal points and currency symbols will be lined up in a column, potentially making it easier to interpret data.

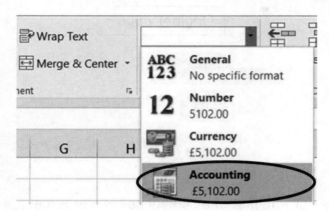

In our example, if we once again highlight cell B3, go into the number options drop-down, but this time select 'Accounting'

The resulting format will be as shown below:

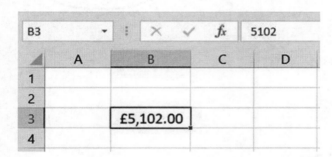

4.4   Percentage

This enables numbers to be displayed with a '**%**' symbol at the end, and also multiplies the value in the cell by 100.

For example, if we type 0.1 and 0.5 into cells, and then select '**Percentage**' formatting from the drop down menu:

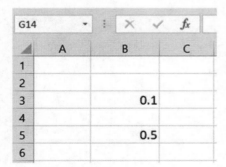

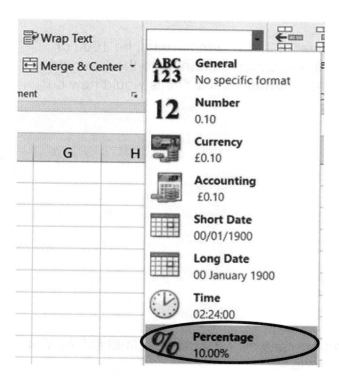

The result will be that the decimal values are changed to their equivalent percentage values, of 10.00% and 50.00%:

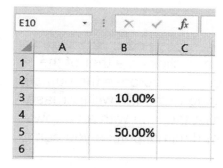

4.5   Thousand Separators

The thousand separator is an excellent way of making numeric data easier to read.

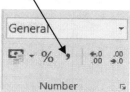

If you click on a cell with a number in it (the number must be 1000 or more), this will insert a thousand separator. Returning to the example of 5102, with the thousand separator format selected, this would now be shown as:

B3	▾	⋮	✕	✓	*fx*	5102	
◢		A		B		C	D
1							
2							
3				5,102.00			
4							

4.6 Decimals

The decimal places option lets you select how many decimal places you would like your answer provided to.

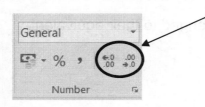

You simply select the cell you wish to change, and click on either of the icons depending on whether you wish to increase or decrease the number of decimal places. The icon with an arrow pointing to the left will increase the number of decimal places you can see, whilst the icon with an arrow pointing to the right will decrease the number of decimal places you can see.

Suppose we wanted to show the previous value 5,102.00 to only one decimal place; we would click on cell B3 and then click the below icon (with the arrow pointing to the right) once, to reduce the decimal places from two down to one:

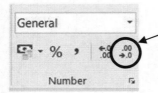

IMPORTANT NOTE ON FORMATTING!

It is worth noting that changing the number format of a cell HAS NO EFFECT on the actual number within the cell. For example, if the cell contains the value 15.6, and you change the format to zero decimal places, the value of the cell used in calculations will still be 15.6, even though 16 will be displayed.

5 Using formulas

5.1 Simple calculations

Excel's primary purpose is to manipulate raw data through calculations and formulas. One of the main things you will use Excel for is simple calculations. The most basic calculations are the mathematical functions addition +, subtraction -, multiplication * and division /.

To use these, you need to tell Excel that you are using a **FUNCTION**. To do this, enter an equals sign, '=', before the calculation you require. So, to find the answer to 3+5, type in any cell:

=3+5 and press **Enter**.

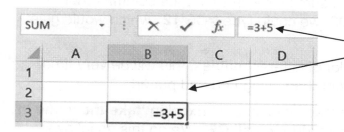

As you type, the formula is displayed in the formula bar, as well as on the spreadsheet itself.

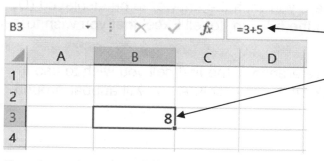

Once enter is pressed, the result of the calculation is shown on the spreadsheet, but the calculation itself is still shown in the formula bar.

Excel can be used in this way as a simple calculator by entering the calculation required, using +, -, * or /.

> **⬤ Test your understanding 4**
>
> Identify which one of the following is the correct formula to enter if you wished to find the solution to 10 multiplied by 20.
>
> **A**   @10*20
>
> **B**   =10+20
>
> **C**   '10*20
>
> **D**   =10*20

5.2 Calculations using existing values

The real power of Excel comes to the fore when using the values in other cells as part of your calculations. Consider the following example:

	A	B	C	D
1	Name	Hours worked	Hourly pay	Gross wages
2	Ibrahim	35	£12.00	
3	Muller	37	£14.00	
4	Williams	40	£13.00	
5	Kuma	36	£14.50	

We need to calculate each person's gross wage, which will be the hours worked (column B) multiplied by the hourly pay rate (column C).

We could do this by typing the sum in the gross wages column (D). For example for Ibrahim, in cell D2, we could type **'=35*12'**, which would give us the value 420.

However, where there are a lot of different entries, this will be very time consuming and not much better than using pen and paper!

What we can therefore do instead, is to instruct Excel to **'take the value in cell B2 and multiply it by the value in cell C2'**. We do this as follows:

- Firstly, select the cell where you wish the answer to be displayed (D2 here) and begin by typing the **'='** sign, to tell Excel that you wish to perform a calculation.

- Next, either type the cell reference of the first cell you wish to use (which is B2 here) or click on the cell itself. A box will appear around the cell as follows:

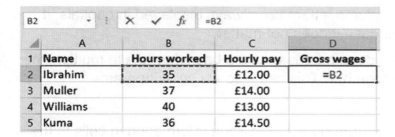

- Next, we need to choose the calculation that is required, using either
  +, -, * or /. We need a multiplication in this example and so would
  type in *

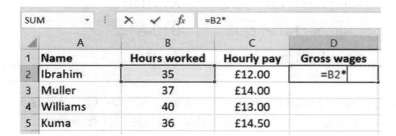

- Finally, we need to select the other cell which is being used in the
  calculation. In this example, it is the value in cell C2 that we wish to
  multiply B2 with. We would therefore either type in 'C2', or click on
  cell C2 to select it:

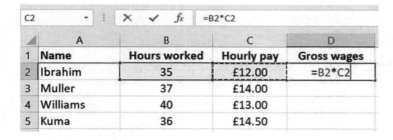

- When we press 'enter', the resulting value will appear in cell D2 as
  showing below. Note that the formula used within the calculation can
  still be seen in the formula bar:

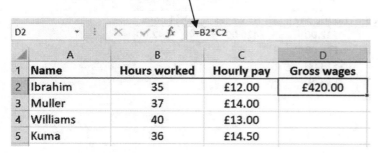

Note that although the column letters are always displayed in capitals, if you enter them in lower case it does not matter.

What we have therefore done here is to use a basic formula to multiply the values within two cells together. This can also we be written as:

=number1*number2

Any calculation can be performed using existing information in cells in the same way as has been demonstrated above (see table below).

Function	Formula	Example
Addition	=number1+number2	=A1+B10
Subtraction	=number1-number2	=B10-A1
Division	=number1/number2	=A1/B10

This allows complex analysis to be undertaken relatively easily. One huge benefit of this is that if the numbers in the data cells change, for example the hourly rate or the hours worked, then the calculation for the final pay will be updated to reflect this.

You can use any cell within your worksheet in the same way. For example, if we wanted to calculate the value of a 10% bonus on the gross wages in our previous example, we could do this as follows:

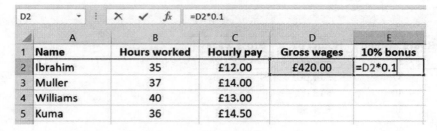

Which gives:

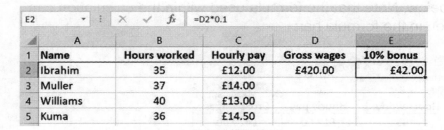

If we then wanted to find the total gross wages in column F, including the bonus amount, we could add together the values in cell D2 and E2 by typing '=D2+E2' into cell F2:

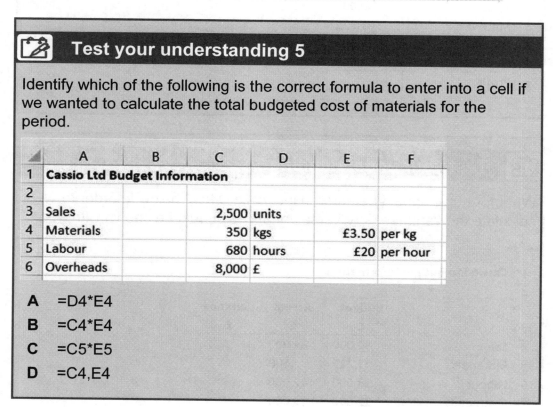

	A	B	C	D	E	F
1	Name	Hours worked	Hourly pay	Gross wages	10% bonus	Total
2	Ibrahim	35	£12.00	£420.00	£42.00	=D2+E2
3	Muller	37	£14.00			
4	Williams	40	£13.00			
5	Kuma	36	£14.50			

Test your understanding 5

Identify which of the following is the correct formula to enter into a cell if we wanted to calculate the total budgeted cost of materials for the period.

	A	B	C	D	E	F
1	Cassio Ltd Budget Information					
2						
3	Sales		2,500	units		
4	Materials		350	kgs	£3.50	per kg
5	Labour		680	hours	£20	per hour
6	Overheads		8,000	£		

A   =D4*E4

B   =C4*E4

C   =C5*E5

D   =C4,E4

Test your understanding 6

What formula should be entered into cell B8 below in order to calculate the budgeted profit for the period?

	A	B
1	Cassio Ltd Budget Information	
2		
3		Budget £
4	Sales	30,000
5	Materials	1,225
6	Labour	13,600
7	Overheads	12,000
8	Profit	

 Test your understanding 7

What formulas should be entered into cells D4:D7 below in order to calculate the variances? Adverse variances should be shown with a '-'.

	A	B	C	D
1	Cassio Ltd Budget Information			
2				
3		Budget £	Actual £	Variance £
4	Sales	30,000	34,000	
5	Materials	1,225	1,500	
6	Labour	13,600	12,000	
7	Overheads	12,000	13,000	
8	Profit	3,175	7,500	

Test your understanding 8

What formula should be entered into cell E4 in order to calculate the percentage variance on sales?

	A	B	C	D	E
1	Cassio Ltd Budget Information				
2					
3		Budget £	Actual £	Variance £	Variance %
4	Sales	30,000	34,000	4,000	
5	Materials	1,225	1,500	- 275	
6	Labour	13,600	12,000	1,600	
7	Overheads	12,000	13,000	- 1,000	
8	Profit	3,175	7,500	4,325	

Test your understanding 9

What formulas should be entered into cells C9, E9 and F9 in order to calculate the weekly basic wage, bonus and gross wage for the employee showing below?

	A	B	C	D	E	F
1	Cassio Ltd Budget Information					
2						
3	Budgeted output	5,000	units			
4	Labour hours per unit	2.5	hours			
5	Hourly labour rate	£15	per hour			
6	Bonus paid per unit	£0.50	per unit			
7						
8	Employee	Hours worked	Basic wage £	Units completed	Bonus £	Gross wage £
9	J. Mumby	37		120		

5.3   The SUM function

In section 5.2 above, we started to perform simple calculations within Excel.

There are also specific words which we can use to tell Excel to perform certain functions. For the purpose of your Principles of Costing assessment you will only need to use the **SUM** function.

SUM is probably the most commonly used function in Excel. As the name suggests, it is used to add up (or find the sum of) a selection of numbers.

Consider our wages example above, and suppose that in cell F2 we now wish to use the SUM function to add together the gross wages and bonus for each employee. We would do this as follows:

- As mentioned previously, to enter a function into a cell, always start with an **EQUALS SIGN** first.

- Then type the **NAME** of the function followed by an **OPEN BRACKET**. This will prompt excel to ask for the numbers you wish to add together:

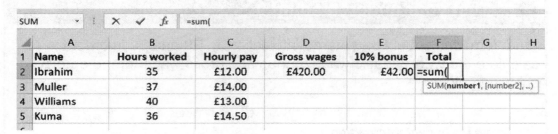

number1 is highlighted in bold showing that Excel is expecting you to enter, or click on, the first number here.

- Click on the first number you wish to use (so D2 here)

- If you wish to add together two or more numbers, you must separate each with a comma, clicking on the second number immediately after the comma (E2):

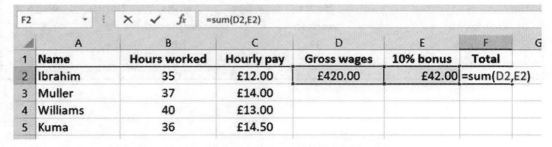

- The function is ended with a **CLOSE BRACKET**.

| F2 | | × | ✓ | fx | =SUM(D2,E2) | |

	A	B	C	D	E	F
1	Name	Hours worked	Hourly pay	Gross wages	10% bonus	Total
2	Ibrahim	35	£12.00	£420.00	£42.00	£462.00
3	Muller	37	£14.00			
4	Williams	40	£13.00			
5	Kuma	36	£14.50			

For example, typing

=SUM(3,5)

will return the value 8. You can do this for any number of additions, and it is no different to using **+**, as in section 5.1.

SUM is really useful when you have many numbers to add up. Consider our previous example:

| H6 | | × | ✓ | fx | | |

	A	B	C	D	E	F
1	Name	Hours worked	Hourly pay	Gross wages	10% bonus	Total
2	Ibrahim	35	£12.00	£420.00	£42.00	£462.00
3	Muller	37	£14.00	£518.00	£51.80	£569.80
4	Williams	40	£13.00	£520.00	£52.00	£572.00
5	Kuma	36	£14.50	£522.00	£52.20	£574.20

Suppose we now wish to put a 'Total' figure at the bottom of column F, to find the total of all wages paid. Using the methods already discussed, we would either type:

=F2+F3+F4+F5

Or

=SUM(F2,F3,F4,F5)

Neither of which is ideal – nor would it be practical if we had a list of hundreds of numbers to add up. Fortunately, Excel has an easy solution – rather than referring to an individual cell, we can refer to a **RANGE** of cells.

We want to add the block of cells from F2 to F5, and would write that as **F2:F5** (the **:** indicating a range). Our **SUM** would be:

=SUM(F2:F5)

Enter this equation as follows:

- Type **'=sum('** in the cell in which you want the total to appear (cell F6 here)

- Left-click (and hold) on the first cell you wish to include (F2). Note the formula is updated:

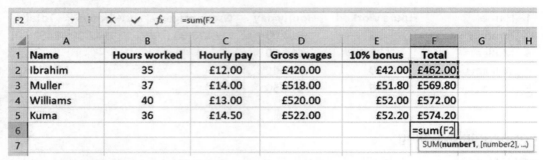

- Drag the mouse down to the last cell you wish to include (F5 here). The box around the cells gives a visual display of the cells selected:

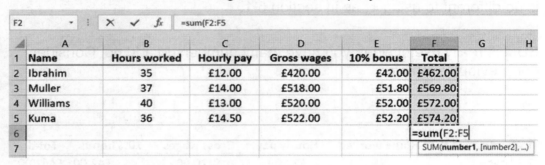

- Release the mouse button and press **Enter** to finish the formula. The correct answer will be shown:

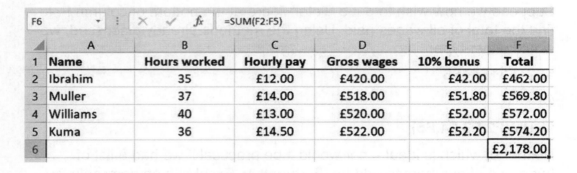

Test your understanding 10

What formula has been entered into cell D8 in order to calculate the total variance in the period?

	A	B	C	D	E
1	Cassio Ltd Budget Information				
2					
3		Budget £	Actual £	Variance £	Variance %
4	Sales	30,000	34,000	4,000	
5	Materials	1,225	1,500	- 275	
6	Labour	13,600	12,000	1,600	
7	Overheads	12,000	13,000	- 1,000	
8	Profit	3,175	7,500	4,325	

6 Summary

The PCTN syllabus requires learners to understand and be able to use different tools and techniques which will support cost calculations. Using such tools and techniques means that calculations can be performed more quickly and accurately than if they were done manually.

This chapter has used Excel to demonstrate the different formatting tools and formulas that you may be required to use as a part of your PCTN assessment. Remember that in your assessment, you will be presented with an interactive screen for the completion of these tasks, which may not be identical in layout/functionality to Excel. However, this chapter has covered the key skills that you will need and you should be able to apply your knowledge of these different areas within your assessment.

Your ability to perform well in these tasks relies not only on the ability to effectively use a spreadsheet, but also on your understanding of the syllabus content that we have covered in chapters one to six. You could be asked to perform cost calculations manually to enter into the interactive screen, and then alter the format of the solution according to the instructions given. Or you could be asked to perform calculations using formulas. Therefore please make sure that you have practiced some exam standard questions on this area as a part of your revision.

Test your understanding answers

 Test your understanding 1

The correct solution is D.

Cell ranges are represented by the value in the top left cell in the range (A3) down to the bottom right cell in the cell range (D5).

 Test your understanding 2

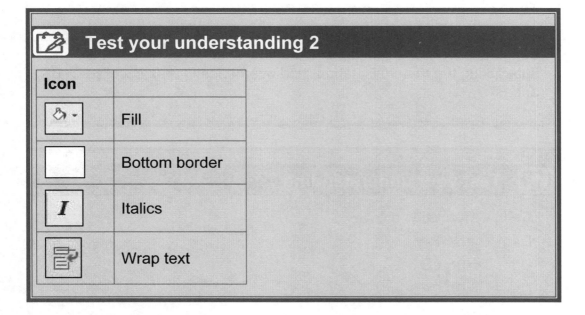

Icon	
	Fill
	Bottom border
I	Italics
	Wrap text

 Test your understanding 3

The correct solution is C.

 Test your understanding 4

The correct solution is D.

Test your understanding 5

The correct solution is B.

To calculate the total budgeted cost of materials we would need to multiply the total number of kgs of materials (cell C4) with the cost per kg (cell E4).

 Test your understanding 6

The correct solution is: =B4-B5-B6-B7

To calculate the profit we need to subtract the budgeted costs from the budgeted income. This means taking the sales revenue in cell B4 and subtracting the materials, labour and overheads figures in cells B5, B6 and B7.

 Test your understanding 7

Cell	Formula
D4	=C4-B4
D5	=B5-C5
D6	=B6-C6
D7	=B7-C7

Tutorial note

For the variance calculations you need to remember to set up each formula so that favourable variances are positive and adverse variances are negative.

This means that for revenue, if the actual revenue is greater than the budgeted revenue, this is a favourable variance and you will take the cell with the actual revenue in (C4) and subtract the cell with the budget (B4).

However, for costs, if the variance is favourable then this means that the budget was greater than the actual. You will therefore need to take the cell with the budgeted value in and subtract the cell with the actual value in.

Test your understanding 8

The correct solution is: =D4/B4

To calculate the percentage variance you take the variance and divide it by the budgeted figure. You can then format cell E4 to 'percentage' in order for the result to be displayed as a percentage.

Test your understanding 9

	A	B	C	D	E	F
1	**Cassio Ltd Budget Information**					
2						
3	Budgeted output	5,000	units			
4	Labour hours per unit	2.5	hours			
5	Hourly labour rate	£15	per hour			
6	Bonus paid per unit	£0.50	per unit			
7						
8	**Employee**	**Hours worked**	**Basic wage £**	**Units completed**	**Bonus £**	**Gross wage £**
9	J. Mumby	37	=B9*B5	120	=D9*B6	=C9+E9

The basic wage is found by multiplying the number of hours worked (in cell B9) with the hourly pay rate (in cell B5).

The bonus is calculated by reference to the number of units produced. This is therefore the number of units produced in the week (in cell D9) multiplied by the bonus per unit of £0.50 (in cell B6).

Finally, the gross wage will be the sum of the basic wage (C9) plus the bonus (E9).

Test your understanding 10

The correct solution is: =SUM(D4:D7)

MOCK ASSESSMENT

TASK 1 (8 marks)

This task is about classification and relationship of costs.

(a)   **Identify whether the following statements are true or false.**

Statement	True	False
Financial accounts must be presented in a format specified by regulation.		
Management accounts may include future forecasts.		
Financial accounts help with internal decision making.		

(3 marks)

(b)   **Classify the following costs by function for a mobile phone manufacturer.**

Description of Cost	Production	Administrative	Distribution
Salary of factory supervisor			
Purchase of camera lenses			
Electricity bill for lighting in the accounts department			
Fuel for the delivery vehicles			
Insurance of the factory machinery			

(5 marks)

TASK 2 (10 marks)

This task is about costing techniques.

(a) **Identify the labour costing methods described below using the drop down list.**

Labour costs are calculated by multiplying a basic rate by the number of items produced, supplemented by an additional amount if production exceeds a certain level.	PICKLIST
Employees are paid for the hours that they spend at work, regardless of the amount of production or output that they achieve in that time.	PICKLIST
If an employee's earnings for output produced in the period are lower than the guaranteed amount then the guaranteed amount is paid instead.	PICKLIST

Options for picklist:

Piece rate
Time rate
Piece rate with bonus
Piece rate with guarantee
Time rate with overtime

(3 marks)

Bounce Ltd manufactures trampolines.

Production staff are paid £25 for each fully assembled trampoline.

In the previous week 1,200 trampolines were fully assembled, with the following costs (in addition to the labour cost mentioned above):

Direct materials   600 kgs at £18 per kg

Production overheads   £30,000

(b) Complete the following table to show the total cost and the cost per unit at a production level of 1,200 units. Overheads are absorbed on a per unit basis. Enter answers to the nearest whole pound.

	Total cost £	Unit cost £
Direct materials	GAPFILL	9
Direct labour	GAPFILL	25
Overheads	GAPFILL	GAPFILL
Total cost	GAPFILL	GAPFILL

(6 marks)

(c) In a manufacturing business that is labour intensive the most appropriate overhead absorption method would be:

PICKLIST

Options for picklist:

Per unit
Per labour hour
Per machine hour

(1 mark)

TASK 3 (8 marks)

This task is about classification and relationship of costs.

(a) Identify which type of responsibility centre is being described in each of the following scenarios using the drop-down list.

Quality control department	PICKLIST
HR department	PICKLIST
Production director wages	PICKLIST
Sales division	PICKLIST

Options for picklists:

Cost centre
Profit centre
Neither

(4 marks)

Happy Toys Ltd, a traditional wooden toy manufacturer, uses an alphanumeric coding system to allocate costs as outlined below. Each code has a sub-code and so each transaction will be coded as a six-character reference.

Activity	Code	Sub-class	Sub code
Sales	SAL	Rocking horses	100
		Teddy Bears	200
Production	PRO	Wood	110
		Wages	210
		Leather	310
Administration	ADM	Telephone	220
		Wages	216

(b) **Code the following transactions for the project, using the coding system above.**

Transactions	Code
Leather costs	GAPFILL
Teddy bear sales	GAPFILL

(2 marks)

(c) **Identify whether the following statements related to coding systems are true or false.**

Statement	True	False
Coding systems prevent errors being made when posting invoices.		
Coding systems make comparisons of similar expenses easier.		

(2 marks)

TASK 4 (10 marks)

This task is about calculating overhead absorption rates and looking at the behaviour of costs.

Digitech Ltd is considering how to cost the various products it makes. It needs to decide on the overhead absorption basis it will use.

(a) **Complete the table below to show the three overhead absorption rates that Digitech Ltd could use. Enter all values to two decimal places.**

	Per machine hour	Per labour hour	Per unit
Overheads (£)	360,000	360,000	360,000
Activity	120,000	30,000	50,000
Absorption rate (£)	GAPFILL	GAPFILL	GAPFILL

(3 marks)

(b) **Complete the table below to calculate the total unit cost of product GT3. Use each of the three overhead absorption rates you calculated in (a). Enter all values to two decimal places.**

Each unit of GT3 takes 6 minutes of machine time and 20 minutes of labour time to produce.

	Machine hour (£)	Labour hour (£)	Unit (£)
Direct cost	27.50	27.50	27.50
Overheads	GAPFILL	GAPFILL	GAPFILL
Total unit cost	GAPFILL	GAPFILL	GAPFILL

(6 marks)

(c) **Which of the three overhead recovery methods would best be suited to a production line where items are hand made by highly skilled craftsmen / women?**

PICKLIST

Options for picklist:

Machine hours
Labour hours
Per unit

(1 mark)

TASK 5 (12 marks)

This task is about calculating costs of products and using tools and techniques to improve presentation.

Good Life Ltd manufactures lawnmowers and is putting together the manufacturing account for its top-selling product, the 'Robo Lawn'.

Using the information provided:

(i) Enter the correct options for cells in column A using the list provided.

(ii) Calculate the values in cells B7, B9, B12 and B15.

(iii) Increase the size of the text in cell A1 to 15.

(iv) Underline the contents of cell A1.

(v) Fill cell B15 with any colour.

(vi) Format cells B2:B15 as 'accounting' to nil decimal places

	A	B
1	**Good Life Ltd: Manufacturing account**	£
2	Opening inventory of raw materials	4,000
3	Purchases of raw materials	24,000
4	Closing inventory of raw materials	6,000
5	Direct materials used	22,000
6	Direct labour	18,000
7	PICKLIST	GAPFILL
8	Manufacturing overheads	46,000
9	PICKLIST	GAPFILL
10	Opening inventory of work in progress	5,000
11	Closing inventory of work in progress	11,000
12	PICKLIST	GAPFILL
13	Opening inventory of finished goods	12,000
14	Closing inventory of finished goods	25,000
15	PICKLIST	GAPFILL

Picklist options:

Cost of goods sold
Manufacturing cost
Cost of goods manufactured
Direct cost

(12 marks: 8 – accounting, 4 – spreadsheets)

TASK 6 (12 marks)

This task is about labour and inventory calculations.

Fantail Ltd had the following movements of inventory during the first half of May.

	Receipts		Issues	
	Quantity (litres)	Total cost (£)	Quantity (litres)	Total cost (£)
1 May	6,000	62,400		
6 May	8,000	84,800		
16 May	4,000	43,200		
29 May			10,000	

(a) (i) **Complete the table below for the cost of issue and closing inventory values of SL3 to the nearest whole pound.**

Method	Cost of issue on 29 May (£)	Closing inventory as at 31 May (£)
FIFO	GAPFILL	GAPFILL
LIFO	GAPFILL	GAPFILL

(4 marks)

(ii) **Identify whether the following statements are true or false.**

Statement	True	False
In times of rapidly increasing prices FIFO will give a higher profit figure than LIFO.		
FIFO does not adhere to IAS 2 and should not be used for financial reporting of inventory values.		

(2 marks)

A company pays its employees a basic rate of £12 per hour for a 35 hour working week (Monday to Friday).

Any overtime during the week is paid at time and a half (basic pay + 50%).

Any weekend working is paid at double time (2 × basic pay).

(b) (i) Calculate the basic pay, overtime and gross pay for the week for an employee working the hours shown below showing all values to the nearest whole pound.

Hours worked Monday to Friday	Hours worked at the weekend	Basic pay £	Overtime premium earned during week £	Overtime premium earned at weekends £	Gross pay £
36	10	GAPFILL	GAPFILL	GAPFILL	GAPFILL

(4 marks)

The company is considering changing the current time-rate method to a piecework rate and paying £3 per completed unit, with a minimum guaranteed weekly wage of £600.

(ii) Calculate the piecework wages for the two employees below for the previous week.

	Units produced	Piecework wages (£)
Employee 1	254	GAPFILL
Employee 2	197	GAPFILL

(2 marks)

TASK 7 (20 marks)

This task is about budget calculations and exception reporting using formulas.

You are the management accountant at Porcelain Ltd, a company which manufactures teapots. You have been provided with the following budgeted and actual information related to the previous month.

Reporting policies state that variances in excess of 5% of budget are significant and should be reported to the department manager.

(a) **(i)** **Complete the table below using formulas in cells B10:E12. Show negatives as '-' or '()'. Enter monetary values to the nearest whole pound.**

(ii) **Identify whether the variances are significant or not using the dropdown lists in cells F10:F13.**

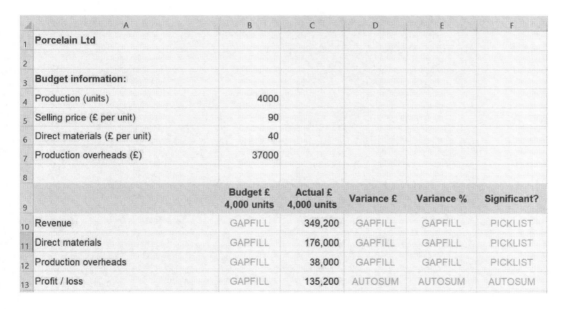

	A	B	C	D	E	F
1	Porcelain Ltd					
2						
3	Budget information:					
4	Production (units)	4000				
5	Selling price (£ per unit)	90				
6	Direct materials (£ per unit)	40				
7	Production overheads (£)	37000				
8						
9		Budget £ 4,000 units	Actual £ 4,000 units	Variance £	Variance %	Significant?
10	Revenue	GAPFILL	349,200	GAPFILL	GAPFILL	PICKLIST
11	Direct materials	GAPFILL	176,000	GAPFILL	GAPFILL	PICKLIST
12	Production overheads	GAPFILL	38,000	GAPFILL	GAPFILL	PICKLIST
13	Profit / loss	GAPFILL	135,200	AUTOSUM	AUTOSUM	AUTOSUM

Picklist options:

Yes
No

(17 marks: 13 – accounting, 4 - spreadsheets)

(b) **Identify whether the following statements are true or false.**

Statement	True	False
A company that has an adverse variance on sales has received less income than budgeted.		
An adverse materials price variance could be due to paying less for each kg purchased.		
Variances help managers with decision making.		

(3 marks)

2 Mock Assessment Answers

TASK 1

(a)

Statement	True	False
Financial accounts must be presented in a format specified by regulation.	✓	
Management accounts may include future forecasts.	✓	
Financial accounts help with internal decision making.		✓

(b)

Description of Cost	Production	Administrative	Distribution
Salary of factory supervisor	✓		
Purchase of camera lenses	✓		
Electricity bill for lighting in the accounts department		✓	
Fuel for the delivery vehicles			✓
Insurance of the factory machinery	✓		

TASK 2

(a)

Labour costs are calculated by multiplying a basic rate by the number of items produced, supplemented by an additional amount if production exceeds a certain level.	Piece rate with bonus
Employees are paid for the hours that they spend at work, regardless of the amount of production or output that they achieve in that time.	Time rate
If an employee's earnings for output produced in the period are lower than the guaranteed amount then the guaranteed amount is paid instead.	Piece rate with guarantee

(b)

	Total cost £	Unit cost £
Direct materials	**10,800** (W1)	9
Direct labour	**30,000** (W2)	25
Overheads	**30,000**	**25** (W4)
Total cost	**70,800** (W3)	**59** (W5)

(W1) Direct materials total cost = 600 kgs × £18 = £10,800

(W2) Direct labour = £25 per unit × 1,200 units = £30,000

(W3) Total cost = direct materials + direct labour + overheads = £10,800 + £30,000 + £30,000 = £70,800

(W4) Overhead per unit = total overheads/number of units = £30,000/1,200 = £25 per unit

(W5) Total unit cost = £9 + £25 + £25 = £59.

(c) **In a manufacturing business that is labour intensive the most appropriate overhead absorption method would be per labour hour.**

TASK 3

(a)

Quality control department	Cost centre
HR department	Cost centre
Production director wages	Neither
Sales division	Profit centre

(b)

Transactions	Code
Leather costs	PRO310
Teddy bear sales	SAL200

(c)

Statement	True	False
Coding systems prevent errors being made when posting invoices.		✓
Coding systems make comparisons of similar expenses easier.	✓	

TASK 4

(a)

	Per machine hour	Per labour hour	Per unit
Overheads (£)	360,000	360,000	360,000
Activity	120,000	30,000	50,000
Absorption rate (£)	**3.00** (W1)	**12.00** (W2)	**7.20** (W3)

(W1) Machine hour absorption rate = £360,000/120,000 hours = £3.00/hr

(W2) Labour hour absorption rate = £360,000/30,000 hours = £12.00/hr

(W3) Per unit absorption rate = £360,000 / 50,000 units = £7.20/ unit.

(b)

	Machine hour (£)	Labour hour (£)	Unit (£)
Direct cost	27.50	27.50	27.50
Overheads	**0.30** (W1)	**4.00** (W2)	**7.20**
Total unit cost	**27.80**	**31.50**	**34.70**

(W1) 6 minutes of machine time = 6/60 hours

Machine hour overhead = 6/60 × £3.00/hr = £0.30

(W2) 20 minutes of labour time = 20/60 hours

Labour hour overhead = 20/60 × £12.00/hr = £4.00

(c) Which of the three overhead recovery methods would best be suited to a production line where items are hand made by highly skilled craftsmen/women?

Labour hours

TASK 5

	A	B
1	**Good Life Ltd: Manufacturing account**	£
2	Opening inventory of raw materials	£ 4,000
3	Purchases of raw materials	£ 24,000
4	Closing inventory of raw materials	£ 6,000
5	Direct materials used	£ 22,000
6	Direct labour	£ 18,000
7	**Direct cost**	£ **40,000**
8	Manufacturing overheads	£ 46,000
9	**Manufacturing cost**	£ **86,000**
10	Opening inventory of work in progress	£ 5,000
11	Closing inventory of work in progress	£ 11,000
12	**Cost of goods manufactured**	£ **80,000**
13	Opening inventory of finished goods	£ 12,000
14	Closing inventory of finished goods	£ 25,000
15	**Cost of goods sold**	£ **67,000**

Workings

Direct cost = £22,000 + £18,000 = £40,000

Manufacturing cost = £40,000 + £46,000 = £86,000

Cost of goods manufactured = £86,000 + £5,000 - £11,000 = £80,000

Cost of goods sold = £80,000 + £12,000 - £25,000 = £67,000.

TASK 6

(a) (i)

Method	Cost of issue on 29 May (£)	Closing inventory as at 31 May (£)
FIFO	**104,800** (W1)	**85,600** (W2)
LIFO	**106,800** (W3)	**83,600** (W4)

(W1) Issues made from the oldest inventory first, starting with the 6,000 litres purchased on 1 May and the remaining 4,000 litres from the purchase on 6 May:

	Cost per unit £	Total cost £
6,000 litres on 1 May	£62,400/6,000	62,400
4,000 litres on 6 May	£84,800/8,000	42,400
10,000 litres		104,800

(W2) Closing inventory = total cost of purchases less cost of issue

Total cost of purchases = £62,400 + £84,800 + £43,200 = £190,400

Closing inventory = £190,400 - £104,800 = £85,600

(W3) Issues made from the newest inventory first, starting with the 4,000 litres purchased on 16 May and the remaining 6,000 litres from the purchase on 6 May:

	Cost per unit £	Total cost £
4,000 litres on 16 May	£43,200/4,000	43,200
6,000 litres on 6 May	£84,800/8,000	63,600
10,000 litres		106,800

(W4) Closing inventory = £190,400 – £106,800 = £83,600

(ii)

Statement	True	False
In times of rapidly increasing prices FIFO will give a higher profit figure than LIFO.	✓	
FIFO does not adhere to IAS 2 and should not be used for financial reporting of inventory values.		✓

(b) **(i)**

Hours worked Monday to Friday	Hours worked at the weekend	Basic pay £	Overtime premium earned during week £	Overtime premium earned at weekends £	Gross pay £
36	10	**552** (W1)	**6** (W2)	**120** (W3)	678

(W1) Basic pay = 46 hours × £12 = £552

(W2) Overtime premium during the week = £12 × 50% = £6 per hour

Overtime hours during the week = 36 hours – 35 hours = 1 hour

Premium during the week = 1 hour × £6 = £6

(W3) Overtime premium at the weekend = £12 × 100% = £12 per hour

Overtime hours at the weekend = 10 hours

Premium at the weekend = 10 hours × £12 = £120

(ii)

	Units produced	Piecework wages (£)
Employee 1	254	**762** (W1)
Employee 2	197	**600** (W2)

(W1) Piecework wages = 254 units × £3 per unit = £762.

(W2) Piecework wages = 197 units × £3 per unit = £591. This is below the guaranteed weekly wage of £600 and so the guarantee will be paid instead.

TASK 7

(a)

	A	B	C	D	E	F
1	Porcelain Ltd					
2						
3	Budget information:					
4	Production (units)	4000				
5	Selling price (£ per unit)	90				
6	Direct materials (£ per unit)	40				
7	Production overheads (£)	37000				
8						
9		Budget £ 4,000 units	Actual £ 4,000 units	Variance £	Variance %	Significant?
10	Revenue	360,000	349,200	- 10,800	-3.00%	No
11	Direct materials	160,000	176,000	- 16,000	-10.00%	Yes
12	Production overheads	37,000	38,000	- 1,000	-2.70%	No
13	Profit / loss	163,000	135,200	- 27,800	-17.06%	Yes

Workings

		Budget £ 4,000 units	Actual £ 4,000 units	Variance £	Variance %	Significant?
9						
10	Revenue	=B4*B5	349,200	=C10-B10	=D10/B10	No
11	Direct materials	=B4*B6	176,000	=B11-C11	=D11/B11	Yes
12	Production overheads	=B7	38,000	=B12-C12	=D12/B12	No
13	Profit / loss	=B10-B11-B12	135,200	- 27,800	-17.06%	Yes

(b)

Statement	True	False
A company that has an adverse variance on sales has received less income than budgeted.	✓	
An adverse materials price variance could be due to paying less for each kg purchased.		✓
Variances help managers with decision making.		✓

An adverse materials price variance could be due to paying MORE for each kg purchased.

Variances help managers with planning and control.

INDEX

A

Absorption rate, 129

Active cell, 192

Administrative costs, 17

Aims of management accounting, 3

Authorisation, 159

AVCO features, 62

AVCO (weighted average), 57

B

Batch costing, 142

Bonus cap, 109

Bonus schemes, 105

Budgetary control, 158

Budgeting, 158, 159

Buffer inventory, 76

C

Calculating gross pay, 98

Causes of variances, 173

Coding systems, 29

Communicating, 3

Communication and co-ordination, 159

Control, 4

Controlling, 3

Co-ordinating, 3

Correction of variances, 174

Cost accounting, 4, 5

Cost card(s), 34, 128

Cost centre(s), 7

Cost classification, 16
    by behaviour, 21
    by element, 18
    by function, 16
    by nature, 19

Cost codes, 30

Cost of sales, 16

Cost unit, 6

Costs of having inventory, 73

D

Decision making, 4

Depreciation, 17

Different types of inventory, 54

Direct and indirect labour, 98

Direct costs, 19

Direct materials, 55

Distribution costs, 17

E

Economic order quantity (EOQ), 76

Evaluating the significance of a variance, 168

Evaluation, 159

F

FIFO (first in, first out), 56, 57
    features, 62

Financial accounting, 2, 5

Finished goods, 55

Fixed budgets, 159

Fixed costs, 22, 136

Fixed overheads variances, 174

Flexible budgets, 160

Forecasting, 159

Formatting cells
alignment, 199
borders, 198
fill, 198
font, 197
merge, 200
wrap text, 199

Formatting numbers, 203
accounting, 204
decimals, 206
percentage, 204
thousand separator, 205

Functions of inventory, 73

G

Group bonuses, 107

H

Historic costs, 2

Holding costs, 73

Hourly rate employees, 99

I

Identifying cost behaviour, 26

Indirect costs, 19, 20

Indirect materials, 55

Individual bonuses, 106

Inventory control, 73, 75
methods, 76

Investment centre, 8

L

Labour, 18

Labour costs, 98

Labour variances, 174

LIFO (last in, first out), 56, 57

LIFO features, 62

M

Management accounting, 2, 5

Management information, 3

Manufacturing accounts, 65, 70
Cost of goods manufactured, 68
Cost of goods sold, 69
Direct cost, 67
Direct materials used, 66
Manufacturing cost, 68

Material variances, 173

Materials, 18, 54

Motivating, 3

Motivation, 159

O

Ordering costs, 74

Other costing systems, 141

Output related pay, 103

Overhead absorption rate, 129
labour hour basis, 131
machine hour basis, 133
unit basis, 129
Overheads, 128

Overheads, 18, 20

Overtime, 100
payment, 100
premium, 100

P

Payment by results, 103

Period costs, 35

Piece rate with guarantee, 104

Planning, 3, 4, 158

Product costs, 35

Production cycle, 54

Production overheads, 128

Profit centre, 8

Purpose of cost codes, 33

R

Reasons for budgeting, 159

Reorder level, 76

Reorder quantity, 76

Reporting variances, 171

Revenue centre, 7

S

Salaried employees, 99

Sales variances, 173

Semi-variable costs, 24

Service costing, 142

Sources of information, 112

Spreadsheet structure, 192

Spreadsheets
    cell ranges, 194
    cells, 192
    columns, 192
    copy and paste, 196
    entering data, 195
    formatting cells, 197
    function, 207
    Inserting and deleting content, 196
    rows, 192
    selecting multiple cells, 193
    selecting single cells, 192
    simple calculations, 207
    SUM, 214

Stepped costs, 23

Stock-out costs, 74

T

Text alignment, 199

Time related pay, 99

Total and unit costs, 136

V

Valuing raw materials, 56

Variable costs, 21, 136

Variances, 165, 173

W

Weighed average (AVCO), 56

Work in progress, 55